PHILIP YORKE
Last Squire of Erddig

PHILIP YORKE
Last Squire of Erddig

Geoffrey Veysey

Philip Yorke — Last Squire of Erddig
© 2003 Geoffrey Veysey
© Typesetting and layout Bridge Books

ISBN 1-872424-21-X

Published in Wales by
Bridge Books
61 Park Avenue
Wrexham
LL12 7AW
on behalf of the author

CIP Data for this book is available
from the British Library

Cover illustration courtesy of the *Daily Mirror*

Printed and bound by
Interprint Limited - Malta

Contents

Illustrations

All the illustrations in this book are reproduced courtesy of the National Trust Erddig Collection held by the Flintshire Record Office, Hawarden, Flintshire

Acknowledgements

I am grateful to so many people for their help and their recollections of Philip Yorke: Elizabeth Pettitt and the staff of the Flintshire Record Office for producing the Erddig MSS in the search room and for their interest in the project; Charles Pugh and Edward Holland, Historic Buildings Representatives of the National Trust (North Wales), and Jeremy Cragg, the House Manager at Erddig, for allowing me to examine the exhibition on Philip on display in the house.

Mrs Dilys Jones of Pentre, Chirk, kindly permitted me to borrow the tapes she had made of Philip's lectures at Marchwiel. Mrs Margaret Owen of Pickhill Bridge Farm shared her memories of Erddig over lunch. I also benefited from conversations with Mrs Helen Banks of Chirk, Mrs Margaret Morgan of Drefechan Farm, Penycae, and Canon Clive Southerton of Prestatyn. Mr Henry Rintoul of Elphinstone Tranent, East Lothian, gave me details of Philip Yorke's entry in the 1937 edition of *The Spotlight*. Mrs S. E. Alman (Wrexham), Mrs Keris Bates of Hightown, Wrexham, Dr John Forbes of Pontblyddyn, Mrs Patricia Hughes of Eyton, Mrs Diana Lewis of Acrefair, and D. J. Taylor of Rhewl, Mostyn, responded to my appeal for recollections, and I am particularly grateful to Frank Thornton of Barnes, London, for sharing with me his memories of his tour with Philip Yorke's theatre company in Ireland in April 1940.

Bill Pritchard very kindly read the text and suggested some improvements. I am also grateful to Rebecca Morgan of Drefechan Farm, Penycae, for letting me borrow the sketch she made of Philip Yorke, her godfather.

The National Trust allowed me to use documents and to select photographs from the Erddig archives, while Alister Williams has been helpful with the preparation and publication of this book.

Geoffrey Veysey
July, 2002

Philip Yorke on his bicycle at Erddig, c.1973. [Courtesy of the Daily Mirror*]*

Introduction

It is more than twenty years since the opening of Erddig by the Prince of Wales and 1998 was the twenty-fifth anniversary of the gift of the house and estate by Philip Yorke, the last Squire, to the National Trust. It is also more than twenty years since the death of Philip himself. His presence is still felt by visitors in the house to this day. One National Trust volunteer had written to him three years before his death 'somehow I cannot think of a place like Erddig belonging to an organisation; to me it will always be your house.'

I have always been captivated by the personality of Philip Yorke after first meeting him during a Chester Archaeological Society excursion to Erddig in July 1971. I recall members of the party clambering up above the attics to inspect the leaking roof and Philip's ingenious array of plastic pipes and buckets to deal with the problem. The entire visit was a joy. Here was someone I considered to be one of the last of the great eccentrics and his death, only seven years later, was a great loss.

After our first meeting I had been allowed, as archivist for Clwyd County Council, to borrow some of the large collection of documents from the house for listing at the record office in Hawarden. Philip at this time was involved in the negotiations with the National Trust, and the parcels of correspondence were duly returned to Erddig. When the Trust eventually assumed responsibility for the house and estate, all the correspondence and papers from one of the best documented houses in Britain were deposited on indefinite loan at Hawarden. They were quickly listed and have been available for research by members of the public for some years. Everyone who consults them must be grateful to the Trust for its public-spiritedness and generosity in making the documents available in this way.

When the house was eventually opened to the public in 1977, a selection of the family archives including many items illustrating the varied life of the house's last owner were put on display in the Tribes Room. The exhibition proved to be so popular that it remained there in some form for several years. Few visitors to the exhibition could have been aware beforehand of the details of his bewildering life which, according to the preacher of the sermon at his memorial service, was 'unusual even beyond the description of eccentricity'. During his lifetime he had been an ordinand, actor, theatre-company manager, soldier, schoolmaster, farmer, tour operator, holiday courier, as well as spending short spells as a school groundsman, security guard, taxi driver and companion. He had also found time to be a keen scout and a church lay reader.

Someone has written that 'man's most enduring memorial lies in the memories of family, friends, pupils … who never met the dead but have heard or read their stories'. They live on in 'a great network of memories that can last down generations and centuries'.

It is the intention of this short biography to present an account of the life of this lovable man which, together with a selection of his articles and short stories, will give an indication why the last Squire will be remembered as long as Erddig endures.

Early Years

Philip Yorke was born on 23 March 1905, the second son of Philip and Louisa Yorke of Erddig. He was christened Philip Scott, his second name after his mother's family, on 2 May. His elder brother, Simon, was the heir and had been born on 24 June 1903. According to his mother's unpublished autobiography, her second son was a 'big fellow with large blue eyes and red hair' like his mother, who always said of him that he was going to be cheerful and contented, and this proved to be the case in later life. Both brothers, neither of whom were to marry, inherited in turn a house and small estate which had been in the possession of the Yorke family since 1733. The inheritance passed from father to son, named either Philip or Simon, the two family names, until 1966 when the last Squire inherited Erddig from his brother, Simon. It was Merlin Waterson who noted in *The Servants' Hall, a Domestic History of Erddig*, published in 1980, that the 'Simons all tended to be, if decent, rather dim and dull. The three Philips (since 1733) were decent; but rarely dull and certainly not dim.'

Their father, Philip Yorke II (1849–1922), as a young man had been described as 'most good natured and docile.' According to his wife, he had suffered as a child from St. Vitus Dance which only disappeared on the approach of adulthood. He unfortunately made a disastrous first marriage in 1877 to Annette, eldest daughter of Sir Richard Puleston of the neighbouring Emral estate. After only a year of marriage, his wife (and her maid), left him early one morning while staying with friends, it is said, by hitching a lift on a milk cart. She never returned. Philip was devastated, and thought he could look forward to 'lifelong misery and loneliness'. He was so hurt by the gossip and innuendo that he left Erddig to travel around Europe and the Middle East with his sketching book.

His wife's death in 1899 released him and he married again in April 1902 at the age of 53, Louisa, daughter of Revd T. J. Scott of Chilton Ffoliot, Wiltshire, at one time chaplain of Malaga in Spain. Mrs Yorke spoke Spanish as a child and lived there until the age of twelve, so that her younger son's attraction to that country and its people all his life is not difficult to understand.

The Yorke family, c.1907.

Philip Yorke senior was described by his son as 'an eminent Victorian who painted pictures and rode a tricycle'. Indeed he enjoyed bicycling with his wife. So much so that they spent their honeymoon cycling and they often undertook long journeys together, Philip cycling to Coventry in a trip which took six hours with 43lbs of luggage. Mrs Yorke confided in her diary that they were always cycling and that she got 'very tired and hot'. Their lives were spent making 'visitations', and leaving calling cards on their friends and neighbours. They maintained the Yorke tradition of hospitality to an almost reckless degree. Mrs Yorke had a total of sixty-five guests to stay during 1920 for example. Like his ancestors, Philip had a taste for amateur versifying and wrote for every occasion, even going so far as to place verses on boards throughout Erddig woods. With his wife they formed an unconventional couple and were not typical of their Edwardian neighbours.

However, both parents were devoted to their two sons who were brought up in a house famous for its eighteenth-century furniture and collection of servants' portraits, and in a family which had little interests outside Erddig. It was their son, Philip, who was to break out of this tradition. Few improvements had been made to the house before Philip senior inherited it in 1894. An income of less than £5,000 p.a. had to provide for an indoor staff of 15 servants and maids, together with 5 outdoor staff.

As ready money was scarce, Mrs Yorke often undertook much of the household work herself, repairing the saloon curtains and the library carpet while tackling the woodworm in the state bed with thymol and paraffin. The situation became difficult following the death of her husband in 1922. Mrs Yorke lived through the rigours of the Second World War, and died at the age of eighty-seven in April 1951. She kept a diary for almost seventy years and these small volumes are now among the Erddig archives. She was an avid patron of the Wrexham cinemas and

Philip Yorke II on stilts at Erddig.

Philip as Cupid in September 1911.

theatre, and regularly walked to Wrexham to attend church services until she was over eighty-five.

The young Philip went to St. Fillan's Preparatory School, Heswall, and later Moorland House School, also in Heswall. Both brothers were educated there, but Simon was then sent to Cheltenham College, while Philip left Moorland to become a boarder at Shrewsbury School in Michaelmas term 1918. At Shrewsbury he developed an interest in rowing (he obtained 2nd House Boating Colours), and played in the Officers' Training Company band on 'the French horn, cornet, bombardon, and other queer instruments.' He was secretary of the school's Darwin Society, but the minute book shows six blank pages for his period of office. He enjoyed a 'fairly unremarkable school career', his teachers noting that he possessed 'a good intelligence and a nice disposition', but had not yet 'developed a taste for books'. The Headmaster concluded in one of his reports that 'his tastes are rather those of the field than the study'.

At his housemaster's recommendation, he was sent in September 1922 to stay with the Dean of Hereford, paying fees of seven guineas a week to be coached in Classics and French for university entrance. Needless to say, the Dean considered Philip's Latin to be 'hopeless'. As a past headmaster of Cheltenham College, he had known and despaired of his brother Simon who had an even more undistinguished career, being taken away from Cheltenham because his work was not up to standard, and having to sit his Cambridge entrance examination six times before passing. Philip eventually went up to join him at Corpus Christi College in October 1924.

Erddig had already begun its inevitable slow decline after the death of their father in 1922. Mrs Yorke agreed to give up £200 of her housekeeping money so that they could afford to pay for a part-time agent. Expenditure invariably exceeded income, but an indoor staff of fifteen was still retained and the size of the overdraft usually prompted Mrs Yorke to invite the bank manager to lunch. There were obvious difficulties in keeping staff on comparatively low wages, to work in what was rapidly becoming an antiquated house and a run-down estate.

Everyone had hoped that Simon's inheritance on the death of his father would lead to a 'great <u>revival</u> of the Erddig prosperity' with 'hopes declared for happy marriages for the boys to <u>ladies</u> with some money.' This was not to be. Both Simon and Philip disliked parties and dancing, so they regularly declined all the invitations they received. In addition Simon's 'desultory and slack ways', and obvious unwillingness to face up to his responsibilities and to tackle the problems facing the estate caused concern, and soon had their effect.

While at Cambridge Philip rowed in the college boat (he was Secretary of the Boat Club), and at Henley. He was chosen for the university trial boat and was in the Final Fours. During the General Strike he drove a railway engine between Willesden and Broad Street Station.

He graduated in 1927 and entered Ridley Hall in July to train for the priesthood.

From an early age he had expressed a wish to enter the Church. At

Cadet Philip Yorke (front right) at Shrewsbury School OTC Camp.

Ridley Hall, Cambridge in 1928. Philip is last on the right in the second row holding a stuffed bird.

university he had sampled all the sects in turn, attending their services. He came from a religious background; daily family prayers were held in the chapel, and his parents were regular churchgoers. The Bible was one of the few books he kept by his bedside table and he had an extensive knowledge of its contents.

He wrote an Old Testament drama in three acts, *A Sacrifice for Sin* which featured David and Jonathan, but there is no evidence of a public performance. His own personal religious views expressed in his Bible stories and sermon notes which have all been preserved, were decidedly odd and highly individualistic. He disliked the teaching of St. Paul and suggested that Barabbas might be the author of the epistle to the Hebrews, his name having been corrupted or possibly altered by the Apostles to Barnabas. He invented his own religion, based on an entire theory of scapegoats, which he called Barabbasianism and which was remembered by his fellow ordinand course colleagues, one of whom later became Bishop of Truro. He also maintained, for example, that

Solomon was 'one of the most brainless men in all history. So conscious of his stupidity was he that he admitted himself that he did not know how to go out or come in — so stupid he gave the baby to the wrong girl'. However one of his ordained friends considered his collection of Biblical portraits to be 'extraordinarily naive' and 'lacking in human sympathy'. He wrote disapprovingly of Philip's 'cynicism and merriment' and his 'debunking narratives' of the Bible's great men and events.

Philip was very popular at Ridley Hall concerts playing in a band he had formed of a 'piano, violin and some of the queer instruments that he was so fond of'. However he passed only the first part of his ordination examinations, and the Ridley Hall Principal did not recommend him continuing his studies 'as he must eventually be taken for other qualities than intellectual'. He is said to have disagreed about the curriculum and objected to learning Greek. He wrote to the college in July 1929 terminating his studies, as he was now busy with a profit-sharing scheme for about 100 unemployed workers at his brother's brickworks which would 'fulfil his desire to have a taste of commerce before ordination.' He continued to attend church services all his life. He took holiday relief sevices although he was never a licensed lay reader. In later years he confined himself to reading the lesson at the churches he attended. The plaque erected to his memory in Marchwiel parish church records that he was a 'loyal churchman'.

Philip, the undergraduate.

Philip and the Theatre

Philip had always been interested in the theatre. His family had been involved in amateur dramatic productions in the Wrexham area, and Philip took part in a church production of the *Bishop's Candlesticks* in Minera and Esclusham in October and November 1929. In 1930 he joined the Northampton Repertory Theatre Company which included actors such as Max Adrian, Noel Howlett, and James Hayter, who were later to make their names on the London stage. James Hayter remained a friend, and he and his family were to spend two holidays with Philip at Erddig in the 1960s before he moved to live in Spain.

A journalist who interviewed Philip for the programme notes at Northampton confessed that he had never met 'so undefined a subject', but found him to be 'an extraordinarily interesting character, very conscientious, very meticulous and somewhat mysterious … whose main ideas appear to be aquatic endeavour, an ardent but somewhat somnolent interest in the Church of England, and a vivid interest in the stage.'

Philip appeared in several productions at Northampton including Patrick Hamilton's *Rope*, *The Playboy of the Western World*, Sheridan's *School for Scandal* and George Bernard Shaw's *Candida*. His mother used to travel each week to see him act, a journey of 220 miles. He left in October 1931 to go to the Royal Academy of Dramatic Art (RADA). A colleague at Northampton wrote to his mother that 'we are all terribly sorry Philip is leaving us. It will be a hard gap to fill. It was a sort of 'presence' we hadn't had ever before & couldn't have again. He is so kind, so funny, so entertaining'. However theatrical training in London never materialised, and Philip next appeared with the Arthur

Philip in Ruritanian costume at Bexhill.

Brough Repertory Players at the Leas Pavilion, Folkestone, in February 1932 for the season.

The following year he had formed the Country Theatre (later known as the London and Country Theatre) Players with a group of fellow unemployed but experienced actors and actresses with Old Vic and West End experience, including Frank Newman, Charles Loyd Pack, Dora Pichon and Vera Draffin, a character actress. A bus which had formerly been on the Penycae to Pentre Broughton route was purchased second-

Philip with his Country Theatre Players bus.

hand by Philip for £20 to take first-class professional actors and successful West End plays to the towns and villages in Kent and Sussex, preferably those 'without a cinema' or 'at least a sixpenny bus ride from the nearest town'. All the equipment was packed into a large trailer which was attached to the rear of the bus. Newspapers reported on the Priestleyesque 'Good Companions' atmosphere in the company.

The first performance of this unusual company took place at Elham Ex-Servicemen's Hall in Kent on 24 January 1933 during the coldest week of the year and in the middle of an influenza epidemic. According to Philip's account, 'at the moment darkness fell, the whole village closed up like an oyster in its shell.' There were initially eleven in the company. Takings on the first night amounted to 35s (£1.75). The next performance it had risen to a little more than £2, and later it was not much better. Philip noted 'they moved from failure to failure.' Only a few dirty children turned up to watch the matinees, and on one memorable occasion the only adult at a matinee was a man with a fur collar who had come to read the gas meter! Although audiences did improve and were enthusiastic on several occasions, the company was drastically reduced in many areas with members of the cast doubling several parts, selling tickets, and acting as doorkeepers. The mechanic and the lady from the box office were the first to be dismissed.

Philip always maintained that the bus broke eventually down at Bexhill, and that the company had only intended to stay for a week's engagement. In the event it ended up by enjoying several successful repertory seasons at the old pavilion on the East Parade at Bexhill on Sea from June 1933, and later at the Park Pavilion. The local council built the new De La Warr Pavilion in 1935, capable of providing more sophisticated and lavish entertainment.

Philip's company (P. S. Yorke Productions) had signed an agreement with the old Bexhill Pavilion to provide entertainments 'of a refined character and free from vulgarity' from July to September, on six evenings with two matinees each week. The nine artistes in the company were to divide the receipts, with 45% going to Bexhill. Similar seasons continued untill 1935, with a break in 1936 when the company was temporarily disbanded, although it had enjoyed seasons also at Bournemouth, Brighton, and at the Victoria Hall in Sunderland. It was a happy company with everyone 'eating together for 10s. a week round one landladily table and Philip talking, talking & showing his personality over the floats instead of acting'. A further agreement was signed with the Bexhill Corporation in March 1937 for an 11 week season at the Park Pavilion, Bexhill, with 30% of the profits allotted to the corporation and £70 a week to the licensee.

Philip was actor, producer, and manager of the company, which put on two popular plays each week with the minimum of cost. The first season included productions of Noel Coward's *Hay Fever* and Frederick Lonsdale's *On Approval*.

By 1937 it was calculated that the company had put on 82 plays, in 450 evening performances and 137 matinees. Plays like Somerset Maugham's *The Circle, Rookery Nook, The Late Christopher Bean, The Ghost Train*, Jerome K. Jerome's *Passing of the Third Floor Back* and Harold Brighouse's *Hobson's Choice* delighted Bexhill audiences who were able to see guest appearances by West End actors such as Walter Horsburgh and Basil Lord. The company occasionally had the services of Henry Ainley as prompter and assistant stage manager while Patrick Cargill, later well known in television comedies, was one of the juvenile leads in a production of *White Cargo* in July 1937. The production costs for *White Cargo* were estimated at 7s. 6d. (37^{1}/2p)

The *Bexhill-on-Sea Observer* commented on Philip's engaging personality and cheery optimism, entirely without pretensions:

Mr Yorke won almost overnight popularity in Bexhill — on stage and off. He was not always word-perfect on Fridays, let alone on Mondays, a

Programmes for the Country Theatre Players

St. MARY'S HALL

WESTERHAM.

PHILIP YORKE PRESENTS

The Country Theatre Players

IN

THE UNFAIR SEX

BY ERIC HUDSON

Tuesday, February 14th, at 8 p.m.

MEET THE WIFE

BY LYNN STARLING.

Wednesday, February 15th, at 8 p.m.

CAST INCLUDES:

Gwen Nelson	Philip Yorke
Vera Draffin	Douglas Bradley-Smith
Dora Pichon	Charles Lloyd Pack
Mary Ramey	Frank Newman

Prices 2/6 and 1/6 Reserved ; 9d. Unreserved.

(Inclusive of Government Tax).

Seats may be Booked at W. T. Williams, High Street.

Kentfield, Tayler & Co., Ltd., East Kent Printing Works

PARK PAVILION, BEXHILL, 1937

8.30 Evenings 8.30   3.30 Saturday, Tea Matinee, Saturday 3.30

★ NO PERFORMANCE ON WEDNESDAYS ★

FOURTH RESIDENT SEASON

PHILIP YORKE

PRESENTS

THE COUNTRY THEATRE PLAYERS

PROGRAMME : Price 2d.   Telephone : Bexhill 1318.

Chandler & Son, 86 London Road, Bexhill. Tel. 550

circumstance that tended to keep the rest of the company on the hop. But the swish of the waves under the Pavilion floor was good cover for the prompter.

Indeed he was so popular that the local rowing club named a skiff after him. It was the same local newspaper which reported his spell of internment in Quebec while on holiday in October 1934. He had arrived there without adequate funds, and deportation papers were about to be served on him. He retained his sense of humour about his predicament and wrote an amusing account of his experiences to a member of the *Observer* staff.

During the company's temporary disbanding in 1936, Philip went off to Spain, and in the winter of 1936/7 also took a month off to work as an underground miner in a South Yorkshire pit. He worked as a filler clearing coal dust created by the cutting machine. He considered the work to be not as strenuous as deep-sea fishermen, and not as monotonous as that of a tube-train driver. Characteristically he was more concerned about the condition of the pit ponies he found underground.

Philip had developed a flair as an actor-manager, and he now formed a new company Philip Yorke Productions with his actress-friend, Gwen Nelson, taking plays to theatres all over the United Kingdom.

Between 1938 and 1940 his company toured Ireland in partnership with Carl Clopet who produced the plays. They included a series of J. B. Priestley plays and tried West End successes (*Dangerous Corner, Time and The Conways, French Without Tears, George and Margaret* and *Pygmalion*). Phyllis Neilson-Terry appeared in several of the productions including *The Scarlet Pimpernel* at Cork and Belfast Opera Houses in 1939. Other guest artists included Catherine Lacey and Cathleen Nesbitt, while Desmond Testor, a well-known boy-actor at the time, starred as Jim Hawkins in the Christmas production of *Treasure Island*.

The young actor, Frank Thornton, joined the Clopet-Yorke company at Thirles, Co. Tipperary, in April 1940 for performances of *French Without Tears* at a salary of £2 10s. per week (£2.50). For this, members of the company were expected to load (and unload) the scenery, take the money and sell the programmes. Thornton remembers Philip Yorke as a 'pleasant eccentric with red hair, pale blue eyes behind spectacles, wearing a brown trilby, grey flannels and bicycle clips, a rucksack, gas mask case minus gas mask, rolled umbrella and, of course, a bicycle. He played the leads with panache unchecked by much consideration for textual accuracy'.

The actors and the Country Theatre Players bus.

Thornton, who was later to be the creator of the memorable character Captain Peacock in *Are You Being Served*, also recalled that at Youghal the company's performances of *White Cargo* were banned by the parish priest.

The outbreak of the Second World War led inevitably to the disruption of the theatre tour, and Philip joined the army. After the war he had a further short period of acting, again with Carl Clopet's company in Cork in 1947, but never re-constituted his own touring company. He had by now moved on to other ventures although he remained in touch with many of the friends he had made in the theatre, particularly Bertram Heyhoe and Gwen Nelson, who periodically came to stay with him at Erddig.

Army Career

On 16 January 1941 Philip went off to enlist in the army at Pembroke Dock, bicycling from Ruabon in the snow with a tiny knapsack. He had been unsuccesful in an attempt to join the Navy two years earlier. He would enjoy a characteristically eccentric career, first as a Lance-Bombardier in a Royal Artillery coast battery at Bexhill-on-Sea of all places, and subsequently as a Sergeant-Instructor in the Army Education Corps based in Northern Ireland. At Bexhill he organised shrimping expeditions in off-duty hours; riding a tandem bicycle, he toured the countryside, studying church architecture and buying chocolates in the Canadian army camps.

The army allowed him to make use of his talents which he had acquired in his now interrupted career in the theatre. Apart from acting, Philip had put together, and was to perform throughout his life, a one-man show involving a selection of conjuring tricks, a recital on the musical saw or euphonium, and comic songs accompanied by himself on the ukelele. In an early letter to his mother he wrote that one of the first questions he had been asked on enlisting was 'about my entertaining qualities, so I had better ask you to send the saw straight away. There is also a peculiar roll of black velvet on a stick & two white gloves in the top left drawer of the big wardrobe in my bedroom; please put them if you can in the same parcel.' A month later Mrs Yorke noted in her diary that she was looking for his trumpet as he was going to give a sing-song in the camp. Philip wrote to a theatrical friend that 'my mother, who is not a great expert at military matters, has a tendency to put on my letters 'Lance-Brigadier' which is anticipating'. He also wrote that 'Mama has gone to Erddig to try and keep away the commandeerers'. Simon had also volunteered and was serving as a signaller.

Conditions in the camp must have been basic, although Philip's only comment seems to have been that the army bed reminded him of the one he had slept on in the Canadian gaol in 1934 'but there was more hot water there.' He was allowed to keep the bicycle he had brought with him to Pembroke, although it was the only one in the camp. In fact he managed to keep three bicycles with him throughout his army career including a penny-farthing, which allowed him to travel around the countryside at weekends and other free time. Philip was to write that 'my bicycle comes first' of all the things which made army life enjoyable for him. He also owned a typewriter, a magic lantern with slides, and a number of musical instruments. He tied his drums to the back of his tandem bicycle, and when he was transferred to Northern Ireland two trumpets and a considerable amount of theatrical equipment moved with him.

His mother called him the'whirlwind' as he periodically descended on Erddig for weekend leave, often with army friends in tow whom he had invited to stay with him. On one occasion Philip went into town with Vera Draffin, a friend from the days at Bexhill, whose mother stayed with Mrs Yorke for long periods during the war. They were searching for salmon, but 'Philip wouldn't wait more than 10 minutes in any of the fish queues & brought back kippers'.

First based at Five Mile Town in Northern Ireland, Philip was responsible for giving lectures on current affairs to serving soldiers. Philip retained his sense of humour throughout his army career which passed comfortably if uneventfully. An article on his work was subsequently published in the *Wrexham Advertiser* in January 1957, while his amusing account on the difficulties of producing a play was obviously based on his army experiences.

He considered volunteering to serve on the continent but eventually decided to remain in Northern Ireland, which suited him 'very well'. He was 'quite glad' to be ordered from his last posting as 'I was down to play the Faery Queen in the pantomime'. He spent Christmas 1944 in cycling around the Mourne mountains and thought his service in the Army Education Corps would be 'a very good apprenticeship for a position as an electrician's second mate' in the post-war world. He won a half-crown for playing the saw and 'had not lectured on sex yet'. He had not seen his partner, Carl Clopet, for five years but was considering writing to him 'to bring what is left of our theatrical company into the district.' A fellow soldier who attended his classes in Ulster remembered him years later as a 'remarkable eccentric':

> At the time, around 1945, there was an American Army film starring Gary Cooper, which was called *Sergeant York,* and was about a rather simple country man who was good at shooting, and who became a great war hero.
> This made Sgt. Philip Yorke seem even funnier and more eccentric. He was in the Army Education Corps in Northern Ireland and gave us wonderfully funny lectures which were really the only bright spot in a

very demanding routine of strict infantry training. He had a completely un-military appearance. He wore his army beret in a totally distinctive & peculiar way. He had a manner of speaking in very educated English, very much like the upper-class chinless wonder but he was very witty and funny. He rode around the barracks on an old tandem bicycle.

During October & November of 1945 he produced a play in which quite a few of us took part. It was called *White Cargo* and was a drama about tropical Africa, which was hilarious fun to do. None of us ever forgot him … .

Philip finally left the Army in November 1946 after a posting to Germany failed to materialise. His discharge certificate referred to his military conduct as exemplary. He was noted as well-read and widely travelled — 'a very fine type of senior NCO who could easily have taken a commission — an excellent teacher and exemplar, a very good organiser who accepts responsibility readily.'

A Variety of Occupations, 1945–66

Before the war, Philip had considered mining engineering as a career, and also had gone so far as to complete an application form to be added to the list of Conservative Party candidates. After his discharge from the army, he toyed with the idea of becoming a civilian instructor at a proposed training centre for army chaplains. He also had a spell of acting in repertory in Cork, Ireland, with his former partner, Carl Clopet. In March 1947 he worked his passage by signing on as a member of the crew of a Finnish cargo boat travelling to Bilbao, Spain. None of the crew could speak English but Mrs Yorke wrote in her diary that 'Phil says they are very nice men.'

Later in the same year he joined the staff of Claysemore Preparatory School near Blandford in Dorset where he taught French and English to the junior pupils. He is still remembered as a 'lovable eccentric' to whom the boys and staff were devoted. Following his popular television appearances in the 1970s in programmes publicizing Erddig, several of his former pupils wrote to him. One army officer recalled:

> Your influence on our young lives at Charlton Marshall was certainly far greater than you ever thought — bikes, churches, peanut butter, songs *On the Lone Prairie, Down the Mississippi, The Walls of Jericho* — French to speak, plays to act, saws to play, and a wide appreciation of life. I think you gave us more real education in your few terms than most schoolmasters in their life time.

His former headmaster considered him an outstanding producer of plays — 'his Toad of Toad Hall I feel certain has never been bettered by any prep school.' Kind and generous, 'in fact one of those rare people a practising Christian' — he regularly cycled the two miles into Blandford on his penny-farthing. He was to remain at the school at intervals until 1953 although he was now spending considerable periods in Spain.

Philip loved Spain all his life from the time of his first visit in May 1924 with his mother and other relatives. He was to make many visits, travelling by bicycle through the towns and villages and exploring the countryside. He often stayed in private houses, living cheaply and accepting rough and ready hospitality from people he met on the road.

For two months in May–June 1949 he drove a 1932 Austin 7 loaded with luggage and a bicycle tied on the back on a 3,500 mile journey through France and Spain with his 85-year old mother, and her friend also in her 80s. Their adventures were recounted in a series of articles printed in the *Wrexham Advertiser.*

Between these visits he had purchased Plas Noble farm at Sontley with 29 acres of land from Lord Kenyon, which a tenant farmed for him. Philip used to stay there on his frequent returns to North Wales. As expected, he was a highly idiosyncratic farmer who plastered the farm with notices — A Feather Bed Farm, Beware of the Cat, AEC Snoopers Welcome. (This was the Agricultural Executive Committee).

By this time he owned several houses in Ruabon. His long-suffering land agent for eight years in the 1950s was Mr Llewelyn Gray, also of Ruabon. It must be said that Philip was a generous landlord who preferred low rents. On one occasion he wrote to Mr Gray that he wanted one of his Ruabon tenants :

> to have a fortnight's free rent and in case they want to take a holiday and even if they are not able to do so because they are saving up to go back to Canada, they will be able to buy candy floss and toffee apples for the children.

He considered his agent took him too seriously and delighted in provoking him:

> I am not worried about money. I have never been better off than now in the whole of my life. My worldly needs are about the level of an unemployed oyster.

In another letter to Mr Gray he wrote:

> in a large clip you will find a fine example of the Yorke method of keeping accounts … . If this sort of account-keeping gives you a headache do not bother even to try and fathom it out but send it on to the accountants as they have learned not to take my affairs too seriously. In the other clip you will find other documents largely concerned with me and the ministry. Also one photo to keep up your spirits. P.S. I shall be at this address until 9 May but I am not at home to the government.

However his agent remained very concerned:

> The business has really worried me lately and it has kept me awake for hours at night. Mr Yorke is such a delightful companion and is kind in the extreme, but his business methods are quite beyond me.

I hate overdrafts for instance, he on the other hand, likes them. Then he has several furnished houses as you know, and he has arranged that the tenants pay their rents into the Bank; some pay properly and regularly but one, in particular, pays short some times and I have not been able to get the bank counterfoil from him and yet Mr Yorke wants to reduce their rent because they are such nice people he says; as a matter of fact the house is very dirty … one tenant drinks a lot and does not pay rent. Mr Yorke says he likes people to drink a lot because it reduces our taxes. Every penny is paid into the bank and yet things are not clear to me; indeed they seem to be in a real mess.

His business affairs were often what can only be described as chaotic. At one time he held four bank accounts 'because in show business one cannot afford to offend anybody, 'together with several overdrafts.

This prompted a letter from one Wrexham bank manager in 1953 that overdrafts at three banks was an unsatisfactory position and 'cannot be justified.'

About this time he offered his farm to Thomas Cook, the travel agents, for possible use by visitors to north Wales. He had a short spell with a bankrupt film company in Spain in July 1952, including some time acting as a watchman on the leading man's yacht then up for sale.

He also worked as a groundsman at Heatherdown School, Ascot, in June 1953. Typically he reported from this last post to his long-suffering agent:

> I have attacked my grass with more vigour than skill, & the whole place has turned brown like the desert portions of Spain. I am told to leave large portions alone for a fortnight, or the whole place may have to be re-turfed.

Another career was to follow, and Utility Tours was set up in November 1953 with Philip as tours manager and driver, operating from Bournemouth. 'Tilly', a grey dormobile, was bought to take 4 or 5 holidaymakers on a three-week inexpensive tour through France and Spain for about '£45, initially at an estimated cost of 2d per mile per person'. The tours usually took place in the spring or autumn to avoid the summer heat, with the itinerary being settled from hour to hour to allow a certain amount of flexibility. When 'Tilly' arrived in a town, Philip left his passengers in a cafe, cathedral, or some other place of interest, while he searched for accommodation. The *Supplementary Suggestions for Utility Tourists* supplied recommendations for the welfare of the holiday-maker passengers:

Philip loading 'Tilly' before embarking on a tour.

Supplementary Suggestions for Utility Tourists

1. Tourists need not be unduly worried if the first few days seem rather expensive. It will be due to France being an expensive country, and the journey being rather long. Most tourists have been surprised, after the first few days, how long their money lasts.

2. Tourists will help the management if they can contrive to get hungry and tired gradually, as it is not always possible to satisfy requirements at a moments notice.

3. The management usually likes to have a break of up to half an hour in the early afternoon. On these occasions, Tourists are encouraged to walk, drink, or sleep.

4. It has usually been found that Spanish towns are more interesting in the mornings, and journeying more satisfactory later in the day. Tourists are especially appreciated if they can find their own interests during their leisure hours.

5. The opinion of the management is usually in favour of those who prefer to press on in France, and to linger in Spain. An interest in architecture, photography, botany, castles, birds, people, markets or drink, is usually an asset.

6. So is a Wilkinson Dry Shaver (obtainable from the Wilkinson Sword Company) for when the water and electricity are cut off.

7. Most tourists bring about 5s. worth of fodder with them for lunch picnics in France, where only bread, cheese and oysters are fairly cheap. This can either be pooled or eaten separately, or if a set meal is preferred, the picnic can take place near a restaurant.

8. Tea, made with warm water and hot milk, can be occasionally obtained at about 1s. a cup. Coffee can generally be got for 4d and wine for 1d or 2d.

9. Single bedrooms usually open on to an air shaft: tourists who are prepared to share have the better choice.

10. The management finds it easier to accommodate the Tourists in the most expensive hotels, and his washing arrangements are then the more sumptuous. Any effort, therefore, that he makes to direct them into cheaper lodgings, is intended to be for the Tourist's benefit. The management sleeps in the 'bus.

It could hardly have been a profitable venture as a number of the clients proved to be his friends, but the first tourists considered their holiday to be a 'most interesting and enthralling experience,' and 'quite blissy'. Only eleven tours were completed (including a few to Scotland), and they finished in November 1955 as Philip's innovatory enterprise was unable to compete with the now emerging holiday tour package companies. 'Tilly' was eventually sold for £25.

Spells of schoolmastering filled the gaps in the next few years, providing some welcome funds. More time was spent in Spain although his bank overdraft, at one time standing at £800, continued to cause him some worry. A film company made a tentative offer to use him and his bus on a production in a minor capacity 'on the production side'. Philip did some taxi-driving, and later taught English to Spanish Air Force Academy cadets in Carthagena. He complained that none of his pupils could understand him but his superiors were impressed, and plied him with bottles of champagne (which he disliked). Again he wrote teasingly to his agent:

> I have issued a general invitation to the Academy to visit me at Plas Noble. There are 250 cadets so if they all arrive together I shall send 50 or so on to you as Simon has no staff and the roof leaks.

He also acted for several months as a companion in Spain to a former Utility tourist, 'a restless old fogey in search of the sun'.

In January 1959 he once again became a courier in Spain, this time joining Horizon Holidays on the Costa Blanca at a salary of £30 a month. He was to remain with them until January 1962, meeting parties of

Philip as a tourist guide in Spain.

tourists at a French airport, usually Toulouse, and accompanying them on coach tours through France and Spain. He proved an efficient and conscientious guide. His managing director thought him to be 'highly erudite' and most caring after his clients. His continental manager at the time (Mr Marnau), remembered him as being 'a man of charm and courtesy and some eccentricity'. It was Mr Marnau, in fact who had to complain of the lengthy, hand-written (but rather amusing) reports which Philip compiled for head office, pleading with him for more concise communications, and for him to obtain some ordinary writing paper so avoiding 'the odd bits of paper and the back of the envelope' which he sometimes used. Philip obviously had a special place in the company, and was allowed several weeks off at the height of the season to attend a wedding and the International Eisteddfod at Llangollen. In one of his last letters he invited his manager to take on a tour himself:

> ... it is a really delightful drive around and you would have the advantage of being able to lay on personally the new scale of tips which has cost you so much mental exercion [sic] of recent weeks. Also I feel that a change of air from the office might do you good.

On his decision to retire from 'the charabancs', he wrote to one of his Utility tourists that:

> ... the passing years make it more difficult to suffer fools gladly and I have had one or two odd customers lately. But my greatest difficulty has always been to try and put a brake on the sharking activities of the French drivers.

Between his visits and work in Spain in the 1950s and early 1960s, he continued to live in North Wales staying at Plas Noble farm or in one of his terraced houses in Ruabon. He toyed with the idea of living in Spain permanently, eking out a living by spending what was left of the family's war loan, or obtaining a post as a guide or teacher of American, or perhaps a relief job on the Spanish broadcasting service 'telling England what a good boy Franco is'.

His brother, Simon, continued to ignore all the signs of the on-going deterioration of Erddig caused by the mining by Bersham Colliery of the Quaker and Main coal seams under the house. The house began to sink and sleep to be disturbed by the noise made by the cracking of the walls. Simon became even more reclusive and difficult. He would not accept any grant for the house's restoration, as much of government money 'has been subscribed by people worse off than himself'. When Philip invited a Ministry of Works official to see Erddig in 1959, he advised him not to arrive using government-supplied petrol 'or you might not be hospitably received'.

Philip tried to persuade his brother to install 20 automated burglar alarms in the house or at least to have a bell or horn, but Simon would not. Rather, he concentrated on buying up land to add to the estate which he let at a low rent of £2 per acre. This figure was doubled if barbed wire was used (which prevented hunting) or if the tenant joined the Agricultural Executive Committee. Visitors (including the postman) were not welcome, and Simon rarely left the house except to go to scout meetings and functions or to cubbing meets early in the morning, riding his bicycle in the dark with a 'pocket of ginger biscuits'.

Certainly the brothers did not agree on the future of the house and estate, but for the time being Simon was the Squire of Erddig. Philip on the other hand was more active and out-going. When he came to live in north Wales and later permanently at Erddig, he began his familiar appearances at village carnivals and fetes, conjuring, rolling a barrel, or playing the euphonium. He regularly played the musical saw for Darby and Joan clubs and Scout shows. At the Darby and Joan club at Coedpoeth he noted in his diary 'they liked my saw-playing of Jim Reeves best'. In late 1964, possibly for financial reasons, he also found time to do a little acting in his former partner Carl Clopet's repertory productions of *Jane Eyre* and *Rebecca*.

Erddig 1966–73

Mrs Yorke just before she died wrote in her diary that 'poor Erddig is going to pieces but Simon is always cheerful.'

Philip inherited Erddig after the sudden death of his brother in May 1966. Simon had died without making a will. He may have been difficult and eccentric but he had succeeded in holding the house and estate together, although the house was falling down about his ears. He refused to deal with the problem, merely deciding to use peat instead of coal to heat the building. In contrast, Philip's colourful life, often living from hand to mouth in foreign countries, had made him adaptable and able to cope with any situation when it arose. One observer noted that Philip was:

> the kindest-hearted and most thoughtful man it has been my pleasure to meet. On the other hand I never in my long life ever met anyone so thoughtless of his own comfort.

He was without fear, and an ideal person to take over Erddig. It was a daunting task but he did not ignore it as Simon had. He may have resented the fact that ownership of a decaying mansion restricted his activities and did not allow him to carry on his previous life style, including his frequent visits to Spain. As he said, he had inherited 'an old house full of eighteenth-century beds and moth-eaten blankets.'

The house leaked in seventeen places as a result of subsidence. Philip told the Coal Board that 'he spent half of my time working for them free of charge.' If Philip can be believed their reply was 'they could think of no way in which my time could be better spent.'

When he moved into Erddig, Philip slept in the drawing room on a camp bed with a cosh on a ledge to hand, and a double-barrelled shot-gun under the bed. He later used a variety of rooms. He could improvise. His burglar alarm consisted of empty evaporated milk tins piled up on a bamboo table resting on a box, and tied with string to a hook on the corridor passage door. Unfortunately it took twenty minutes to reassemble when Philip set it off inadvertently. Although he reported that 'the police were interested in this contraption', yet he felt obliged to add that 'I have no evidence of them setting up another one elsewhere.'

Philip with a group of Scouts at Erddig.

A proper alarm system was later introduced, linked to the local police station.

Simon had refused to have gas or electricity in the house and relied on paraffin lamps. Philip drilled a hole through the drawing room floor and piped up calor gas from the Servants' Hall for himself and his house-guest (Bertram Heyhoe, a fellow actor whom Philip always called Hoo-Ha):

> I put a long board over the mantlepiece with a calor gas mantle at each end. His calor gas mantle was bigger than mine, so I had a £500 silver salver behind his, to reflect the light. My calor gas mantle was smaller, so I had a £1,000 silver salver behind mine, to reflect more light, and I remember saying that they were doing a useful job for the first time in their lives.

When they became dull, his cleaner, Mrs Hughes, polished them up and the light improved. Philip and his guest spent the evenings with their backs to the fire, reading books and listening to a transistor radio.

Philip was more approachable and friendlier than his brother, and this was to be a great help in tackling Erddig's problems. Their mother had noted that Simon does 'no manual work' but Philip always 'worked hard.' He had written at one time:

> that if ever it (Erddig) comes to me I shall welcome every Tom, Dick or Harry to the intimate corners of my home in return for adequate remuneration.

Philip with Trixie in the garden at Erddig.

Inaccessible during Simon's lifetime, there were now streams of visitors asking to see Erddig or to stay in anyone of its twenty-eight bedrooms. The sheets had disappeared over the years, but many guests brought their own or used sleeping bags.

The visitors had many stories to tell. One guest spent a 'complicated night' with two hot water bottles under his mattress and the housekeeper's father's hammer in his bed, which Philip had lost after using it the previous month to repair the west room shutter. Another guest asked to tea in September 1966 was also invited to the cinema. Philip's diary tells that 'he had seen the Wrexham flicks so I tried Rhos, Cefn, Pentre Broughton, all closed, so we came home and played the Chinese national anthem on the Bombardon.' At the Maelor Hospital barbecue held in the grounds, guests toured the darkened house with the help of matches. Philip turned out an Indian doctor twice, by mistake, adding 'I hope I don't fall sick into his clutches.'

The artist who painted a portrait of Philip now hanging in the dining room at Erddig also experienced his hospitality:

I remember being met by Philip at the station when I arrived. The passenger door had no handle and had to be tied up with string. The road was visible through the floor of the vehicle and there were lumps of firewood under the bonnet which were to be given to some impoverished tenant.

Philip and the dog Trixie were the only residents at the time. We were each given a key, to the back door, which was hung about our necks. At bedtime we were handed a candle each and chamber pot and told not to touch the door handles as this would set off the burglar alarm. This, in turn, would summon policemen from Wrexham who would have to be given a drink, and it would all be 'rather tedious.'

The idea of a portrait was introduced. Philip did not at all like the idea but he thought it was his duty to complete the gallery. He agreed to having the painting done, on condition that Trixie was also in it. By the time arrangements had been made for me to paint the portrait Trixie had died — so that her portrait had to be done from sketches that I had made earlier and from a photograph, while Philip sat clutching a cushion on his lap. He had great difficulty staying awake; so we sat in a howling draught and were bombarded with hideous sounds from a radio tuned into Radio 1. (This came on automatically with the lights). The sittings took place in one of the cottages at Ruabon.

Erddig soon resounded to the sound of hammering as Philip and an ever-changing band of helpers made up of a few Erddig workmen, boy scouts, and volunteers, attempted to make immediate if amateur repairs to leaking roofs and the damage caused by overgrown trees. Encroaching beech tree branches on the north wing were tackled with a saw tied to a twenty-six-foot pole — 'the longest in Europe and quite unmanageable' according to its designer. Buildings were falling down everywhere on the estate, and there were problems caused by broken fences and straying sheep and cattle. Philip blamed the trouble caused by the intermittent and occasionally foul water supply firmly on the Coal Board: 'When the river floods we get 3 sewers and the colliery baths to drink.'

Boys were enlisted to paint gates for half-penny a bar for the first and 1d a bar for subsequent gates. Philip had to cope with poachers and 'crowds fishing, taking photographs and being a thorough nuisance.' In his diary he complained of masses of schoolboy helpers and hinderers. On one day in May 1967 he noted he had to deal with '(1) Willy enquiring about the gates at Sontley Lodge (2) boy with spectacles who had fallen in the lake and wanted a boat — lent bathing pants and a towel instead (3) 3 boys looking for a pony cart (4) Miss Lloyd (housekeeper) wanting to go to Wrexham (5) Leech worried about the birds under the roof at Forest Lodge (6) 3 nuns wanting to see the house. I had intended to go to Queensferry to look for a new car but too much on'.

He had the usual problems with mechanical objects — the tractor failing to start, burst tyres, the cement mixer out of action because the previous borrower had left 15 layers of cement in it, or the engine had fallen off. An unsuccessful attempt to burn ivy off the Forest Lodge was interrupted. Philip had gone off to look for mushrooms and 'some ass called 2 fire brigades and a police van.' He later commented in his diary that he felt a 'silly twerp but the Forest Lodge looks much better.' He had no qualms about tackling a leaking pipe at Sontley Lodge — 'unfortunately I made another leak with my spade.' Another tenant complained of a lavatory overflowing at Forest Lodge. The entry in Philip's diary notes that this is 'the first time anyone at Erddig has ever complained of too much water.'

He could not be regarded as extravagant in his own style of living at Erddig. As a 'non-smoking, non-gambling, vegetarian, teetotaller' he estimated that he spent 2s 6d (12p) a day on paraffin for his stove and one ton of coal for his guests. The lack of heating helped to preserve the furniture.

He was undoubtedly aware of his own peculiarities and enjoyed the role of owner of a stately home which he was now called upon to play:

I sometimes ask myself how many families would be prepared to go about on bicycles and broken-down cars and restrict their enjoyment as my family has done for the sole purpose of preserving our heritage intact.

National Trust

Philip was always adamant on what he wanted for Erddig:

> My only interest for many years has been that this unique establishment for which my family have foregone many luxuries and comforts over seven generations should now be dedicated to the enjoyment of all those who have interests beyond the bare necessities of life who may come here and see a part of our national heritage preserved for all foreseeable time.

He wanted Erddig — house, furniture, and park — to be restored and preserved as they used to be.

On his first visit, the chairman of the Historic Buildings Council for Wales, had declared Erddig to be the only thing of its kind in the Principality. Several alternative rescue plans had been discussed at a meeting between Philip and his advisers in October 1966, just six months after Simon's death. These ranged from sale or restoration of the house by Philip himself, acceptance of a grant from the Historic Buildings Council, to offering it to the Treasury who would then pass it on to the National Trust in lieu of death duties. At one stage Philip even offered the house to the Prince of Wales as a country residence in his own Principality, but Prince Charles turned down the gift. The meeting decided to invite the National Trust to discuss the proposals.

Philip did refuse a grant from the Historic Buildings Council for the repair of the furniture, after first enquiring whether the money would have originated from the funds received by the Government following the disestablishment of the Church in Wales. He now began talks with the National Coal Board on the level of compensation to be paid. He allowed Coal Board officials to send their 'crack photographer (to photograph the cracks)', and to install scaffolding to try to put the drawing room stairs back into position.

Negotiations understandably proved long and difficult. Ralph Edwards, a cousin and former Keeper of Woodwork at the Victoria and Albert Museum, was an adviser on furniture to the Historic Buildings Council. He must have been driven to distraction by Philip's actions, and complained that each of Philip's letters contradicted the previous one so that 'you do not seem able to grasp a simple point.'

Philip opposed any suggestion that the furniture not the house be saved, and this 'to be dispersed to other people's houses whose owners have probably sold their own so as to indulge in riotus [sic] living.' If the National Trust did not take Erddig and its furniture altogether, then he would leave it all 'without any conditions whatsoever' to Plaid Cymru, 'and if you can think of anything worse I will give it my consideration.' A series of draft wills and instructions included suggestions for the break-up of the estate to build houses for Pakistanis and West Indians. He even went so far as to draft a letter to Vanessa Redgrave, the actress, asking if she would consent to be one of the trustees to make use of Erddig to house immigrants. The remuneration would be small (£2 for every year of his life at the time of his death), 'but I can think of nobody who would implement it more wholeheartedly'. Another suggestion was for two-thirds of the money received from the sale of the estate to go to the Conservative party, and the remaining third to the Welsh nationalists. All the furniture was to be sold 'preferably in America.' These extreme measures were obviously intended to put pressure on the National Trust to accept his proposals.

Philip eventually signed a Deed of Gift to the Trust on 14 March 1973. Valued at three million pounds, it included the house, furniture, 1, 964 acres of estate land, 14 farms and several houses and cottages in Wrexham and Ruabon which had been part of Philip's personal estate. In a supplemental agreement made the same day, the Trust had also to agree to continue the Yorke custom of allowing the grounds to be used for hunting and for camping, together with other boy scouting activities. Nothing was to be moved from the house, including any pieces of furniture which were to be offered to the treasury in lieu of death duties. The National Coal Board agreed to pay £120,000 compensation to the Trust.

Such a munificent gift naturally received considerable publicity in the national press. The diarist James Lees-Milne, who had done so much to persuade owners of stately homes to convey them to the National Trust after the Second World War, considered it 'one of the most splendid acts of generosity I remember in all the years which I have been associated with the Trust.'

When receiving his benefactor's entrance ticket, Philip expressed pleasure at the gift saying that it was worth every penny: with it 'he could take a friend into any National Trust house in Britain.' The subsequent sale of 63 acres of Erddig Park in the Sontley road area for £995,000 paid for the restoration work on the house, which was only

Above: The Prince of Wales and Philip Yorke at the opening of Erddig in 1977.

Right: The Prince of Wales on a penny-farthing at Erddig.

completed when the house was officially opened to the public by the Prince of Wales on 27 June 1977. Everyone involved in the task of repairing the house and restoring the gardens was invited, and the visitors included workmen and the friends of Philip Yorke from his repertory days, Vera Draffin, Gwen Nelson, and Bertram Heyhoe. A decorated dais was erected in the yard and the Prince took the opportunity to drive the Morris car which had been restored, and also tried his hand at riding one of the penny-farthings, but with little success. As a memento of the occasion he was presented with the watch which had originally been the gift of Queen Victoria to her god-daughter, Victoria, on her marriage to Simon Yorke.

Final Years

As a former actor, Philip showed himself to be a natural performer on television, and his appearances in several programmes on the restoration of Erddig helped to publicize the National Trust's activities. At the same time it greatly increased his already extensive correspondence. In his lifetime he had made and retained an incredible number of friendships. He was by no means a lonely bachelor, and friends he had made in all walks of life now wrote to this lovable and kindly man. They included former Erddig servants and tenants, university friends, members of the Folkestone and Bexhill repertory theatre audiences, as well as old Clayesmore school pupils where he had taught thirty years previously. While the house was being restored, Philip was 'stuck all alone at Erddig after 6p.m. until 9 a.m. the following morning. All day the place is full of National Trust officials … and at 6 p.m. everybody goes somewhere else'. He only had his dog, Trixie, for company. He did not have a high opinion of the National Trust:

> They are completely profligate, and the Yorkes would not have lasted three generations if we had spent half the money that they go in for. Anyway, they have sold the land at a high rate, and things are getting better. The roof is coming on well, and they have put pipes all over the place for the drains. Wrexham Water is in (unnecessary). The telephone people have practically taken up residence here. A clock was sent to the repairers, though there was nothing wrong with it, and the best field (a football field) has been sold for a negligable [sic] sum.'

There were a few disagreements with the National Trust, which he now tended to call the 'National Distrust'. He fell out with the administrator whom he accused of drinking and of locking everything up, including the bicycles. He disliked many of the Trust's decisions. He thought the Stansty gates were sunk too low and should be higher. The Trust had taken the heating out of the chapel, dismantled the play room, and made the dining room pictures appear as if they wanted cleaning. He objected to the pulling down of Orchard Lodge, and other alterations to the estate.

The opening of Erddig meant that he had achieved what he had set out to do. He retained a small flat in the house and also eventually

Philip Yorke on his penny-farthing (drawn by Rebecca Morgan).

moved into a terraced house in Ruabon, which had remained part of his personal estate. There had been talk about going to Spain, Australia or to New Zealand 'where it is not so hot.'

However, once the house was opened, he much enjoyed acting as an unofficial house guide. He knew that he was putting on an act at Erddig:

> I do it so well that people go out of their way to say that I am enjoying myself … I think I will give up talking at Erddig free and concentrate on my lectures. I am told I am ruining my voice.

He continued to lecture on Erddig and Spain to church and village organisations in the locality for charity, using his father's 100-year-old magic lantern and colour slides. He auditioned for ITV's *World of Pam Ayres* programme in July 1977 playing the musical saw which he had bought for 15 shillings out of the *News of the World*, and which he had played for fifty-seven years.

He returned several times to Spain, the last time in the winter of 1977–78 when he toured on a bicycle. He had first called in at Buckingham Palace with two stands for the penny-farthings which he had given to Prince Charles after the opening of Erddig, and which were kept at Balmoral.

He died suddenly on 2 July 1978 at Penylan church at the beginning of a service to which he had arrived hot, flustered, and late. He had set off by bicycle, originally for Marchwiel.

Eccentric to the end, his will dated 29 November 1973, showed a multitude of bequests to old friends, Erddig estate workers, godchildren, and included Lord Kenyon, the Marquess of Anglesey, Ridley Hall, Cancer Research, Shrewsbury School and Chester Rowing Club. He also left bequests to several churches in the Wrexham area(all of which he attended regularly), and to Plaid Cymru, the Conservative Party, the Humane Slaughter Association, and the Distressed Gentlefolk's Aid Association. The Salvation Army received £500 (divided between the Belfast, Bexhill and Wrexham branches) 'in acknowledgment of their helpfulness to me during my war service'.

One of the Last Eccentrics

There are so many stories about Philip Yorke and his eccentric style of living in Wrexham that he has become a legend in the area. According to a recent study, the eccentric is someone who deviates from the unconventional, who knows they are different, and glories in it. Philip certainly did. On one occasion he wrote 'You don't often find someone who suddenly finds himself worth three quarters of a million and does not want a penny of it for himself but only for preservation.'

His mother had noted in her diary that Philip 'likes to be peculiar.' He never bought new clothes, always second-hand double-breasted suits from a Liverpool store, often using safety pins instead of a belt to attach trousers to the shirt. He was usually hatless except occasionally for a beret or crash helmet, and never wore an overcoat. He was certainly not extravagant in his own style of living, and uninterested in food. A vegetarian by choice, he existed on eggs, cup-a-soups, and rich tea or ginger nut biscuits. Shopping was haphazard but he usually stocked up with quantities of the cheap lines on offer in the local store.

He was never without some form of transport, and a succession of motor bikes and cars were treated remorselessly. Many of his cars ended their lives as river blocks to repair damaged streams. His Robin Reliant had a wire through the dashboard which served as the clutch. His cars usually had the passenger seat removed to allow ease of access for Trixie, his pet dog, or to hold quantities of firewood to be given to some impoverished tenant. His motor cycle invariably had the saddle tied on with a piece of string. In his last years he travelled everywhere by bicycle.

He is remembered above all as a lovable man. He kept a balloon in his pocket for use when he met children, and always took a bottle of Ribena on visits to his god-daughter. He was kindhearted, hospitable and generous, with a great capacity for friendship, with no thought of his own creature comforts or of any class distinction. In his colourful life he made and retained friends wherever he went, and his correspondence was extensive. He often sent sums of money to actor friends down on their luck to take a holiday, or loaned money to others. Guests at Erddig found their breakfasts prepared by their hardworking host who also undertook many other duties.

He could not be described as intellectual, and his reading was confined to the Bible which he kept by his bedside, the *Wrexham Leader*, and the two volumes of *Chronicles of Erthig on the Dyke*, his family history. He held many right wing views which he possibly inherited from his mother. He supported General Franco and measures against coloured immigration, maintaining that Socialist intellectuals wanted coloured people in England. He was in favour of Ian Smith's White Rhodesia policy, although he noted that Selwyn Lloyd had been a 'bit dubious' when told of the 'Support Rhodesia' sign he displayed on his farm. He joined the Racial Preservation Society and backed Enoch Powell.

He was in favour of the introduction of decimal coinage as children would learn more quickly, resulting in the reduction of the minimum school-leaving age and 'children will leave school less ignorant than they do at present'.

He could be sharp in correspondence when provoked, although it is more than likely that many of the copies and drafts of his letters in the Erddig MSS were of correspondence never sent, but which gave him an opportunity to vent his feelings. The head postmaster at Wrexham who had alleged that there was no record of a current TV licence at Plas Noble farm or Erddig was accused by Philip of being 'incompetant [sic], careless or dishonest'. Some of the letters written during the protracted negotiations with the National Trust are said to have bordered on the libellous.

Philip Yorke, senior, had hoped that his second son's life would be like a snail's so that 'wherever I go I leave a shiny track behind me'. His son would prefer it to be 'like a Rolls Royse [sic] so that I move swiftly and silently everywhere and leave no track.'

Philip had two quotations which he copied in his diaries. One: 'A gentleman puts more into life than he takes out of it'. The second: 'True happiness lies not in the abundance of material wealth but in the paucity of wants'. He lived by these tenets.

Literary Career

Philip wrote articles and short stories all his life. He completed a play, *Sacrifice for Sin* and wrote several accounts of his travels in Spain. He corresponded regularly with George Lerry, the editor of the *Wrexham Leader*, who encouraged him in his literary endeavours, and who published his Spanish adventures in a weekly series of articles called 'A Wrexhamite in Spain'. They were printed in the *North Wales Guardian* and later in the *Wrexham Advertiser* in the 1950s. Many of the notebooks, drafts and copies of his articles can be found in the Erddig archives.

At one time he offered a selection of his collected work, under the title of 'Spanish Horizons', to *Blackwoods Magazine* in July 1949 but this was rejected, as it was an unedited transcript from tape recordings. A further sample of his writings was collected together for Stockwell Book Publishers after he noted an advertisement from the firm soliciting material in the *North Wales Guardian*. Other compilations were similarly rejected.

At the age of twelve, Philip's schoolmaster had noted in his report that 'in composition he allows his imagination to run away with him from the point at issue'. His spelling was atrocious all his life but this did not prevent him writing articles on a variety of subjects, ranging from The First Attempt to Ascend the Col de Tourmalet in the Pyrenees in 1924, to the Coal Pickets of Sunderland, and Sunday Cinemas.

A keen observation, added to a quirky sense of humour, combined with a developed sense of the ridiculous and absurd to make him a writer of considerable talent.

Among the early compositions was a poem in characteristic Yorke rhyming verse about the college rowing boat, which appeared as an 'Ode to a Friend in Danger' in *The Gownsman*, a Cambridge University publication, in February 1926.

Appendix

This is a selection of Philip Yorke's articles and stories based on his adventures during his Army service and his travels in Spain. It also includes some of his correspondence, with several letters which display his eccentricity.

Brushes with the Law

Some time ago when I had stopped my motor cycle outside the National Provincial Bank, and before I had even put it on its stand, I was ordered by a Police Sergeant to move on, as I was causing an obstruction.

Before me and behind me were immense lorries drawn up against the kerb. I pointed out that they were causing a much greater obstruction than my little old motor-bike, but I was informed that they had a right to be there as they were discharging merchandise, whereas if I remained there for more than five minutes I should be summonsed.

I argued for some fifteen minutes that what I was discharging into the bank was as much value to me as the goods finding their way into Messrs Francis & Woolworth were to other members of the public. But the Police Sergeant just reiterated the refrain 'The magistrates shall decide', while the Wrexhamites looked on. I was rather hoping to have the opportunity of presenting the case for the individual on the second-hand motor bicycle as against the presidence [sic] given to the great combines. But the case was never called.

Some time before that,

Philip preparing to go shrimping.

when I was cycling in London on my Lea-Francis bicycle (1895 variety), I found myself in a head-wind, mounting a considerable incline on the Silvertown Way. A great lorry slowly overtook me, carrying, as it turned out, fifteen tons of grain. I laid my hand gently upon it and almost immediately I heard a loud ringing noise and a luxurious limousine drew up at the public expense. A man in uniform got out and took my name and I was subsequently issued with a summons which stated that I 'did unlawfully take and retain hold of a lorry for the purpose of being drawn'.

I fought the case. I argued that as my bicycle had a fixed gear, and my feet continued to turn while I held on to the lorry, I did not see how the Police could tell whether I was being drawn, or pushing.

The stipendary took a very reasonable view of the case & did not convict. He pointed to my summons and told me to take it away and get it framed. It proudly hangs beside the deportation papers which I won in Canada in 1934 for being 'inflicted with a loathesome disease or likely to become a public charge'.

While the police have been affording me these innocent amusements, I have lost an acre of promising spruce trees, cut down and stolen at Christmas time for the purpose of promoting good will amongst men. I learn moreover that outside my sheltered life in the army, my home, and the school where I am now teaching, deviations from good conduct have been on the increase throughout the length & breadth of the land.

As I shortly hope to use some of my 'basic' in the Wrexham area, I wonder if some of the police could be diverted from the too easy task of catching the fairly law-abiding citizen off his guard, and occupy their business where it might be of rather more use.

D/E/2368

Some not so serious thoughts on
the Army Education Corps

I got the sack from school for ignorance. After I had been in the Army for some time, I felt that I was just the kind of man they needed in the Educational Corps. In these days I understand that a 'failed WOSB' (War Office Selection Board) is usually regarded as the normal qualification.

My application was accepted and I was immediately issued with a new suit of clothes. Then, when I had got rid of the unsightly crease in each trouser leg, and when I had caught a cold which rendered me speechless, I felt that I was ready to take my first ABCA (Army Branch of Current Affairs) period.

The topic laid on for our deliberations was the Atlantic Charter, and a lively discussion ensued covering pay, leave, women and demob. What the soldiers chiefly wanted to know was how to get more pay than you are entitled to, how to get leave before it is due, and how to get out of the Army before the end of the war. As regards women, they knew all there was to know, and simply wanted to tell the others.

I think it was the only completely successful ABCA that I ever conducted. Subsequently, when my voice returned, my sessions deteriorated into a tedious discourse from me, while numbers of my audience slumbered and slept. Having been to some extent educated myself, I was prepared to show an understanding heart towards those who liked to acquire knowledge somnolently through the subconscious mind, but I was always careful to wake up those who snored, even at the risk of disturbing the other sleepers. For this purpose I found the bursting of a paper bag an effective means; the final occasion when this method was used being just as the CO made his appearance with his staff, consisting of Adjutant, Orderly Officer, Regimental Sergeant Major, and so on.

In lecturing, I always worked on the assumption that it was a waste of time trying to tell anyone anything that they did not know already. Newspaper magnates have made fortunes by finding out what the average uninformed members of the public are thinking or want to think, and telling it to them day by day in newsprint. *The Times* makes the mistake of trying to record what the Government is thinking or pretending to think, and its circulation is naturally rather small.

Occasionally it was necessary for us to attend a few lectures ourselves. These usually consisted of showing us how to stress the left wing point of view without seeming to break the rules of impartiality.

Or we might find ourselves taking a class of soldiers, many of whom had attended school for about nine years, and teaching them how to spell words of two letters. Such a curious effect did it have on me that I usually went along to the NAFFI and had a cup of coffee when the class was over, in order to try and make certain that I was not dreaming. But as the NAFFI coffee was so reminiscent of the dull sort of stuff which is usually provided for me when I eat and drink in my dreams, it took me a long time to make sure that I was really awake.

Many of the illiterate soldiers appeared to be well above the average in intelligence. It may have been that faculty which enabled them to get out of learning any more in so long a time. But sometimes if you asked them, shall we say, to treble seventeen and subtract it from 303 by mental arithmetic, they would have the answer before you could say 'Jack Robinson'. And if you saw them in the evening they generally seemed to have found the smartest girls to go to the pictures with.

I remember asking one such soldier on the following morning what the show had been like, and he said that it was one of the rottenest pictures he had ever seen in his life, and what was worse, he had seen the very same picture in the town where he was stationed the week before he had come to join us in our six weeks Basic English Course.

When I asked him why on earth he had gone again if he did not like it the first time he told me that he had gone there by mistake because he was not able to read the title. It may well be supposed that that soldier was a fairly keen student, and like many others before he left, he was able to stumble through a few carefully chosen verses out of St John's Gospel, as a reward for which he received from the chaplain a copy of the New Testament with a picture of His Majesty King George VI on the front page which he proudly put in his pocket, and I often wonder whether he ever bothered to look inside it again.

Opprobrium

At that time I was able to bring down a considerable amount of opprobrium on my head by suggesting that, for the average and sub-average students the time to raise the school-leaving age would be when we had enough schools to place them in, and enough teachers to teach them, and in the meantime they could be set free to go and relieve the shortage of juvenile labour which followed the war. It seemed to me that after nine fairly unsuccessful years of schooling, another consecutive year would not be likely to make very much difference to their scholastic ability, whereas the time to catch up might be, as with the soldier I have mentioned, after they had found out their shortcomings and at an age when their powers of concentration had improved.

But I always felt that it was in the outside activities of educational activities that the instructor was best able to prove his worth. These activities included such things as putting on plays and concerts and obtaining materials for handicrafts. It was found that quite a pleasant profit could be quickly made on leather work for example, at a time when the materials were not available to the general public, and it was thought that even an unmusical instructor, with the help of a few gramophone records could instil a liking for classical music into the frequenters of the Educational Study Centre who had really only gone there to sleep or to listen to the Light Programme while re-thumbing the back numbers of *Men Only*.

For my own part I never found my ignorance of classical music to be the least handicap in this direction, and in fact, on more than one occasion I was able to put it to positive advantage. Quite often, after I had been giving a gramophone recital, some one would come up to me and remark, 'I say, you don't seem to know much about it, do you?' or words to that effect. And this was always the kind of comment that I was most delighted to hear because I saw in it the opportunity of getting my critic to do the work for me the next time.

This in educational parlance was known as 'sub-letting the contract', an art at which I have always regarded myself as something of a past-master. In the days when I used to run a theatrical company, I always said that if ever I had to do any work myself, it was only due to a breakdown in the organisation. It was, in fact, only due to the propensity that so many people had for regarding the provincial repertory manager as something of a supernumerary lay curate, that I was kept fairly busy for a number of years.

Records

I always used to advise any ignorant educational instructor who was down to give a classical recital that it was as well to classify his records into groups of similar subjects by differing composers for comparison, and even to read up some notes relating to the music or to the composers before the recital began. But we seldom did. We were more likely to rush into the record room at the last minute and pull out the records from the alphabetical department which seemed to be best filled, and enter the Study Centre announcing 'Tonight, gentlemen, we are going to hear some carefully selected classical records of which all the names of the composers or the artists begin with the letter 'J'.' The instructor then starts looking through the pile, rather wishing that Harry James or Spike Jones were included amongst the classics, and finding no 'J' he comes to the conclusion that the last person who looked through the records must have put them back in the wrong places.

It goes without saying that an Instructor who can deal enthusiastically with a variety of subjects of this kind will readily make himself indispensable in the cause of modern education. It seemed to me that if only I had known how to run a puppet show, they would have made me a brigadier.

In fact there were times when I used to wonder how the educational activities in my particular region would manage to carry on after I had tendered my resignation. But I have always said that the moment anyone becomes indispensible, that is the time to get rid of him.

The Army Educational Corps was proudly designated the Royal Army Educational Corps just about the very same day that I severed my connection with it. Previously to that I had never entertained a very high regard towards the War Office, and in fact, if they had asked my advice on quite a number of matters, I should have told them to act quite differently from the way in which they did act. Nevertheless, from that time on I was forced to admit that they did at least seem to possess a certain amount of caustic perspicacity.

Wrexham Advertiser, 15 January 1957 (D/E/2368)

Philip (centre) with a group of actors on tour in Ireland.

How to Produce a Play

There is nearly always a fatality connected with amateur dramatics.

When I was a young man, I killed off or maimed most of the charitable workers in my part of North Wales, by no greater effort than an attempt to produce a sketch for the local charity bazaar.

In the army, the dangers are much greater. Besides the normal acts of God, we have complications of man's making which are much further reaching. To overcome these, a fanatical producer should be appointed. He should be as tactful as an ambassador, and as brazen as a temple vessel; he should possess boundless energy, and a bicycle.

A meeting will be held, the play will be cast, and a rehearsal called for a certain time and place. The producer will arrive at that time and place, and will wait for half an hour, before going off on his bicycle to look for the players.

The leading man will be found on Jankers, and after about ten minutes talk with the Provost Sergeant, he is released for half an hour, amid a chorus of disapproval from his fellow-defaulters.

The leading lady will be on a lecture on beauty culture, and after the lecture is over, will be pleased to come, if she has time to get ready.

The rest of the cast will be on night ops, spud-bashing, sick, or posted.

It will then be necessary to inveigle passers-by to come in, in relays, to read supporting parts, so that the leading man can get an idea of what the play is about, before he returns to the guardroom. The leading lady should try and arrive before the rehearsal breaks up, so that a time may be arranged for the next rehearsal (when a similar fiasco will take place) before she adjourns to the NAFFI for the rest of the evening.

Eventually after innumerable trials and troubles, after rehearsals have taken place in the guardroom, in CRS over spud-bashing and barrack-room cleaning; after all the NCOs have been stripped, and the officers posted in a subordinate capacity, after plagues and torments, necessitating the changing of the entire cast about three times, the play nears the time of production.

A dress rehearsal is then called in the gym, for a time when the gym is wanted for something else.

The producer then sets off to solicit the help of the Entertainments Officer, and after he has waited for about an hour in the back premises of the Officer's Mess, while exhaustive enquiries are being made to find out who the Entertainments Officer is, it is discovered that the Entertainments Officer was posted some weeks earlier. It is therefore decided that the dress rehearsal shall take place on the night of the performance, some hours before the performance is due to begin. When the actors arrive, it is found that somebody has spoilt the scenery, so the producer sets off on a bicycle to get some paint and brushes. He is informed in the paint shop that these can only be issued on signiture [sic] from the officer in charge. After half an hour's wait in the back premises of the Officer's Mess, the producer is informed that the officer is not available, so the scenery is abandoned.

It is then found that there are no light bulbs on the stage, as the bulbs usually belong to the dance band, and have been stored away for safety. The producer sets off to acquire a new set, and is informed that light bulbs can only be issued if broken holders are returned in their place. The cast is then sent off to look for broken holders, and to borrow bulbs from the unwilling slumberers on the barrack rooms, and to take them fom the Information Room, and by the time they get back, the audience has started to come in, so the dress rehearsal is abandoned also.

All that the actors now have to do is to set off in the main to try and borrow a wheelbarrow so as to scrounge some coal to light the fires, and it will be found that if it is a free show, some 10 per cent of the unit will attend. Even if a charge of 3d is made, some 5 per cent of the unit may be confidently hoped for.

The play is then performed, and after some obvious criticisms have been liberally made, it is pronounced a success. In fact, some 90 per cent of the unit would have liked to have seen it, if they had known it was on, and understood that it was free.

The producer is then asked to undertake another production immediately, and is promised unbounded support and co-operation in the future, which he immediately accepts; unless he has been in the army for six years, and sees his release date coming into view; then he is steadfast in his determination to have nothing more to do with it whatsoever.

I have heard that a new production is in hand in this unit. It is up to all of us who intend to steer clear of it to give them all sympathy and encouragement (short of actual help) in all the trials and troubles which undoubtedly await them.

D/E/2368

The Railways are to be Nationalised

Most people think it cannot possibly make them any worse than they are at present.

Of course there are a number of people who think that the railways are excellent; they associate them with smart carriages on long distance train journeys, with porters almost servile in their civility and their willingness to oblige. They think of railways as a national necessity, and in terms of the good dividends which they pay.

These are the people who have habitually travelled by motor in the past, and who will mostly travel by aeroplane in the future. Their contact with the railways has usually been confined to a visit to Scotland in the autumn, and a boat-train to the continent in the winter. The ordinary hum-drum traffic which pays the dividends, is a closed book to them.

But not to us.

We know only too well the cold comfort of the blazing fire in the railwayman's cabin, as we kick the ashes in the third-class waiting room. We know the brusque reply we are likely to get if ever we have the hardihood to interrupt the conversation of a group of porters at a terminus, when we want to ask for a direction. We know the inaudible incivility we receive as the icy blast blows our ten shilling note through the window of the booking office when we pay our exhorbitant [sic] fare.

And then we make our way with our luggage to our antiquated trains under the disdainful scrutiny of self-satisfied officials. We arrange ourselves on soiled cushions, and peer with hardened faces out of grime-laden windows at fellow sufferers as they stumble through the gloom, to take their unwelcome places at our side.

The train moves on and we come into the fair countryside, which makes a singular contrast to the derelict appearance of the stations at which we stop. At every station the company has thoughtfully left behind a railway carriage of an earlier generation and robbed of its wheels, now used as a toolshed, in order to imply to present-day travellers, that our for-father's [sic] mode of transport, was no more luxurious than our own.

And if we have the temerity to travel with a bicycle, we come under all the pent-up spleen of the railway employees. We must wait patiently while they unload the fish and parcels, before we are permitted to retrieve our property from the guards van and dash hopelessly over bridges to try and catch some whistling connection on a distant platform. If we request to get our bicycle out quickly, officials will inform us that they do not want bicycles on the trains anyway. As a matter of fact they don't really want anything at all, excepting their salaries. All the stupid regulations which beset railway travellers are purely one-sided, and any idea of the railway companies fulfilling the needs of the travelling public died, if it ever existed, about the time of Queen Caroline.

And now the railways are to be nationalised.

It cannot do them any harm, excepting that with Government support they may continue to exist, instead of dying a natural death, like the Hansom cab.

D/E/2368

The Decay in Perambulators

The magnificence of my early perambulations was enhanced by the elegance of the vehicle in which I travelled. I remember well the two smaller wheels which led the way, and the others, some five times their size which followed. There were curves of ornamented ironwork which led aloft, from which was slung at a perilous altitude the body in which I lay. Upon it was carefully painted in yellow, a basket-work pattern in imitation of the seats of the nursery chairs, and from it rose, in graceful bends, the handle-bars which terminated in glazed china, white as the covering beneath which I lay. Above my head in rainy weather could be raised a hood in white india-rubber with lining of a royal blue, or in bright sunlight, a tasseled canopy, under which my admirers were permitted to peep at the exquisite spectacle within.

But now, when I witness the perambulator parade in Hyde Park, or find myself in contact with a nursery cortege on any of our roads or streets, I avert my eyes from the perpetual sombre blue of these vulgarly shaped vehicles, progressing uneventfully upon their equi-diametrical wheels. The other day, however, in one of the side-streets of London, I saw an object which reminded me of all the glories of my early youth. There was the widely differentiated magnitude of the wheels, though one of the forerunners was gone. The others had long since lost their tyres, and wandered in complaining crawl along the gutter. The bodywork was in a condition of sad dilapidation, but careful scrutiny could still reveal the painted basketwork that once had won the admiration of so many. What was left of the hood hung like the broken wing of some great bird. One side of the handle was adrift, but still there lingered a broken portion of white china that had once been the pride of so smart a nursery maid. The undercarriage was bent out of all recognition of the stately curves it once possessed, but to me, as I looked upon this relic with sympathetic eyes, there seemed to emanate a dignity, unsurpassed by some of the better-known sights of our great city.

But in the place where once my infant ringlets might have rested, a large brass trumpet asserted itself, and instead of my silvered tones, one heard a gutteral voice bewailing 'Where is my Wandering Boy To-night?'

Now I am not usually susceptible to the tragic sights which beset our daily path through life, but on this occasion, I must confess, I thrust my hand deep into my pocket, and, as I passed, drew out my handkerchief to wipe away a tear.

D/E/2952

Craig's Wedding

A friend of mine got married at the Savoy Chapel. I have not been to many weddings so I got there in good time and propped up my tandem in the churchyard. As I am not very conversant with weddings I asked the verger which side of the church the guests of the bridegroom sat, and, being told it was on the right, I found a seat next to a girl in the WRNS.

My friend was rather an eminent American and before long the church began to get full of potentates and foreign-looking uniforms. Someone asked me which side they should sit, & I was able to tell them, friends of the bridegroom on the right, and friends of the bride on the left, but they seemed a little doubtful as to whether I was right.

Then came the bridegroom's American father and took the front pew on the left, and numbers of the guests from the right side got up and changed to the left including the people who had spoken to me, casting an angry glance at me as they pushed past. But the Wren & I held our ground, and the little church started to get very full.

Then came the bride's grandfather who wanted to sit in the front pew on the left & found it occupied by the bridegroom's American father. They had a whispered conversation for some time and eventually the grandfather won & the American father had to change over to the right with his tail between his legs.

Numbers of the guests tried to change over again, but the pews were getting very full & they had to take places at the back.

The Wren grinned at me and asked me if I would share a taxi with her to go to Claridges for the reception. I said I could do better than that & I offered her the back seat on my tandem.

One of the parsons who took the servise [sic] was a relation. He possessed nothing but antiequity [sic] and confidence, and made such funny noises that some of the congregation began to laugh. I pushed my handkerchief into my mouth and nearly swallowed it in my attempts to remain silent, & I felt very ashamed of myself. The man on my right was somewhat overcome, but I comforted him by pointing out that the Bishop in front of me had giggled a bit. He said that he would have unfrocked him if he had'nt.

After the servise [sic] I was amused to see all the uniforms and potentates standing on the pavement, unsuccessfully thumbing for taxis.

The WREN & I sailed past them on the tandem and arrived at Claridges amongst the first of the guests. I asked the Commissioner where to put my bicycle, and he replied 'There is no bicycle park at Claridges', so I propped it against the railings & gave him 6d to look after it. When I came out, someone had taken the pump.

D/E/2952

Mr Buddy

Shortly after I joined the Army Educational Corps I was posted to Fivemiletown in Northern Ireland. There were two camps about two miles apart, Ochintaine and Blessingbourne, and they had previously been occupied by Americans who had recently been posted abroad.

When the camps became empty, a kind lady went round the town to find homes for the various dogs that the Americans had left behind, and a dentist friend of mine, called Len Stansfield (of the same family as Gracie Fields), received a short-haired brown dog of uncertain age and lineage. As Len regarded him as an American he called him Buddy, and he became very fond of him, but Buddy never settled in to civilian life. He spent most of his time sitting on the lawn looking across the road to where one of the camps was situated, and although he conscientiously escorted the patients up the short drive to the surgery and back to the gate, his main interest was listening for the welcome sound of marching men.

When English soldiers took over the camps, most of the dogs rejoined the army as volunteers, and paraded regularly round the cookhouse. Eventually the numbers became so great that the Commanding Officer had to issue orders that any dog who did not actually belong to army personnel would have to be disposed of. Len was worried about Buddy as he knew that it would be impossible to keep him at home while there were soldiers about, so he asked me to sign the papers to say that I was his military owner, and he promised me that the engagement would not be irksome, as Buddy would probably be fed in camp and, if not, he was welcome to drop in at mealtimes at home.

I introduced myself to Buddy and took him unwillingly along to the Administration Office at the other end of a lanyard, and I don't think he ever forgave me for it. We never got to know one another very well as he was essentially an infantryman, and I had to traverse the distance between the two camps on a bicycle. He divided his attentions about equally between the two camps, as I did, and we often nodded to one another if we happened to meet on the road, but that was about the limit of our acquaintanceship. The fact was that Buddy rather looked down on me for going about on a bicycle, while all the best soldiers were marching.

When the troops lined up on the parade ground, Buddy was there, and when they went on a route march he went with them, and if, at the end of it, he saw another contingent setting out as he approached the barrack gates, he unhesitatingly turned about and joined them also. So conscientious was he that he was eventually made into some sort of honorary Sergeant Major, and then of course we all called him Mr Buddy, and on more than one occasion when he had marched himself into absolute immobility, he was granted army transport to take him back to camp. But if there were night-ops to follow, Mr Buddy would be back on the parade ground.

When I was posted to Belfast, I left him without any great feeling of regret as I had hardly got to know him, but I was careful to find a good infantryman to take my place as sponsor, so that Mr Buddy would no longer have to suffer the ignominy of belonging to someone who went about on wheels, and by that time he was so well known that it was not necessary to take him to the office for the ceremony of change of ownership.

I did not hear of him for years until I returned to Fivemiletown on a motor-cycle to revive pleasant memories of the camps, and to see how my friend Len Stansfield was getting on. One memory of Fivemiletown which I had forgotten is that the main street is at the same altitude as the top of the spire of Clogher Cathedral a few miles away. My motor-cycle went wrong at Clogher where there was nobody to mend it, so I had to push it up all the hills to Fivemiletown. When I eventually got there I found that Len had retired and had moved in with his sister somewhat lower down the street. They invited me to stay, and I asked about Mr Buddy.

When the camps had finally been disbanded, Mr Buddy had taken up his duties again as dentist's receptionist, but his heart was never really in the job. He sat in the garden on fine days and in the sittingroom window when it was wet with one ear cocked and his eyes endlessly fixed on where the camp had been, waiting for the sound of marching which never seemed to come. Only when the patients came and went did he relax his vigil to escort them to and from the surgery until months forlornly passed into years without incident; and then one day …

Mr Buddy was sitting by the open window when the sound of marching men was heard again. He was off like a flash and through a hole in the fence, up the road and out of sight. Len waited to see if any troops would arrive and then realised that the sound was getting fainter and fainter until it came to an end altogether. He left some food available for Mr Buddy in case he came back hungry during the night, and after a day or two he began to make enquiries as to whether anyone had heard troops marching or had seen an elderly brown dog with short brown hair wandering anywhere around the countryside, but without result.

It almost seemed as if the sound must have been made by some of Mr Buddy's old comrades and buddies from the camp, and he had gone to join them, marching in the sky.

American papers please copy.

[This story is reproduced by kind permission of the Benchers of Gray's Inn in whose magazine, *Graya*, it was published in 1971.]

Journey to Lourdes

My guide book tells me that Lourdes has a castle which is used as a prison, and that it makes handkerchiefs and woollen stuffs. Since that time a girl called Bernadette saw a vision about which a rather charming film has been made with Jennifer Jones in the leading part, and the aspect of the town has been somewhat changed.

When I got there it was rather wet weather and most of the streets were up and there were piles of mud where they were digging drains or something and all my customers wanted a bath.

I went round to a dozen hotels which all charged four shillings for a bath, and at last I found one where the baths were only two shillings but the accommodation was fairly prohibitive, and the dinner turned out to be rather poor.

And all the time I was prancing over the muddy heaps of earth, and interviewing hotel proprietors, I was suffering considerable inconvenience from a painful ulcer which had been worrying me for some time where a misplaced wisdom tooth was erupting and sticking into the back of my mouth. I had seen my dentist about it in the interval preceding the trip, and he thought that the only way of curing the sore place was to have the offending tooth extracted, but he had not the time to do it then, and suggested that I should either have it done abroad or wait until I next came home.

Since then the discomfort had got worse, but as we had been rushing about I had not had the opportunity of having the tooth taken out, and I wanted to get it done at home on the Health anyway.

When eventually I had made all the arrangements, and my temper was a little frayed, we ran into two American priests on holiday who said that we ought to have been staying at their hotel which was quite comfortable. I inquired the price and found that it was getting on for three pounds a day. One of the Americans, on hearing that I came from Wales, almost accused me personally and the Welsh in general for having been responsible for the execution of Mary, Queen of Scots. My knowledge of history did not enable me either to agree with him or to refute the charge, and on my subsequent research in Lord Birkenhead's book of famous trials, I can find little to support the theory, unless he was referring to the fact that Queen Elizabeth I was a Welsh girl, unless, as is commonly supposed, she was really a man masquerading in disguise.

GROTTO

One of the Americans talked my customers into attending a Mass which he was due to take in the Grotto at half-past-six the following morning, and I had a nasty feeling that I would be expected to run them down there in the bus. So I slipped quietly off and found my way to the Grotto before the procession of blessing the sick was due to start that afternoon. I wanted to see whether the child's artificial leg was still hanging amongst the relics, as I had since heard that prior to the healings at Lourdes, the only authentic place for growing new limbs was at Zaragossa. The leg was gone, and so were many of the crutches which I had remembered seeing on a previous visit when I was a schoolboy. Nearly everything was covered in the thick black of many years of candle smoke.

When I approached the row of holy water taps, I saw a small boy bathing his squint. I watched it for some time to see if it got any better, and then with a considerable accumulation of unbelief I thought it was not likely to do any harm if I had a go at gargling behind my wisdom tooth. I was in process of doing this, with my head tipped back and slightly to the left, when I noticed that the procession had begun. In front came a quartette [sic] of Alsation [sic] girls in the characteristic costume of big black bows and check skirts. Following them were lots of priests of many nations and variations of colour. They were bareheaded and wearing cassocks, and they chanted an incantation as they came. Further down the line were my two Americans. They were taller than the others, and resplendent in their mackintoshes worn over their cassocks, and with plastic covers over their Homburg hats.

The procession had some way to go before reaching the chapel so I took a short cut to join the invalids who were waiting for its arrival, drawn up in four long lines of beds and wheel chairs in the great open space below the chapel steps. As they waited they repeated litanies, sometimes solo, sometimes in unison. After a while, someone started praying through a loud-speaker a little way off. He addressed the Saviour as 'Seignor', but I could not understand, and cannot remember a lot of what he prayed. When he said 'Seignor, someone whom you love is ill,' I felt a little guilty about the lighthearted way in which I had gargled my wisdom tooth.

When the procession arrived the deluge arrived also, and there was a great scattering of invalid carriages and sightseers, and I went off to look at some of the souvenir shops wearing a ground sheet and sou'wester.

There are rows and rows of shops all selling the same commodities at different prices, and some of them have the most inappropriate names.

I stopped at the 'Sacred Heart of Jesus' or some such place, and a sharking woman popped up and tried to sell me an expensive music box. One of my tourists found a shop with the more homely title of O'Toole, and as her own name was O'Toole, she bought a perspex ball containing a Virgin in a golden snowstorm. I eventually bought a shallow drinking vessel in aluminium, with a picture of the chapel stamped on the bottom, partly because it was the cheapest thing in the shop, and partly because I thought it would come in useful for tasting wine in the Spanish 'bodegas'. German and Swiss students who are good at languages seem to earn about enough money as touts in these shops during the summer to pay for their education at home for the rest of the year.

When I was thoroughly dripping, I found my way in the direction of the old town in search of a reasonable meal, and I nodded to my clients who were munching their supper near the window of their hotel as I passed. Most of the dining room windows of the hotels look out on to the street, and in one of the most sumptuous I saw a whole tablefull of rotund ecclesiasts with what looked to me like nothing less than a Cardinal at the head of the table, just finishing a banquet. I had some soup, an omelette and some cheese for about four shilling in a shabby little restaurant among workpeople whose great-grandparents had probably been acquainted with the Saint in person, and then I parked my bus where I could catch my customers for their service in the morning.

The rain woke me up several times in the night and it was at its hardest at six when I heard the steady tramp of hundreds of people with many maimed among them, all wending their way towards the grotto to hear the American Mass. My people thought better of the weather and did not turn up, so I peeped through my curtains until all was quiet and then I went to sleep until the crowd trudged back again.

One notable fact struck me, namely that my ulcer was certainly no worse, and that it even seemed to me that it might be a little better. I thought how nice it would be if only the discomfort abated until I got home again, but after a week or so the pain had quite gone and now as I write five months later, it has not returned. I know of course that I shall have to have the tooth out when a convenient moment arrives, and when I do, I am thinking of sending it to the grotto authorities in the hope that they will hang it up in the place of the artificial leg that they have taken away.

On the other hand I shall be forced to understand their point of view if they decide against it as some of those seeking for faith in the cure of their ailments might find an extracted tooth rather a misleading relic if they have not had the good fortune to be readers of this week's *Wrexham Advertiser and Star*. Moreover the time that a tooth has become blackened by candle smoke it might be more suitable for being exhibited behind a large magnifying glass in the ghost train at New Brighton Tower Gardens, rather than gracing the Grotto at Lourdes.

And now, whenever I think of Lourdes, I shall try and forget the death of poor Mary, Queen of Scots; I shall try and forget the four shilling baths and the sharks in the inappropriately named shops; and I shall try and forget the rotund ecclesiasts at their sumptuous meal. But I shall remember the lines of the sick, and the little boy bathing his squint, the people tramping through the rain to the six-thirty Mass and Jennifer Jones hurrying off to the shrine with her grandmother carrying the candle. I shall remember the prayer 'Seignor, someone you love is ill,' and the fact that the sore place behind the tooth of the unbeliever was miraculously cured.

D/E/2961

A Wrexhamite in Spain

Madrid is a great modern city with masses of new buildings, somewhat over-ornamented, and the water and electricity generally cut off. On the occasions when these commodities are both turned on together, an absolute industry is started of people with baths and buckets and basins taking water up in the lift to the floors where the pressure will not reach. For this reason the visitors generally have to walk; and they are advised to tread delicately because of the slush which accumulates on the landings, and trickles down the slippery stairs.

I met an American in Madrid. I suggested it was probably all right for him, as he was in one of the best hotels. He said that made it all the worse, because big hotels are made with plenty of dark places lighted from a wick floating in olive oil, an invention left over from the times of the Roman occupation. He was paying 12s. 6d. a day for his bedroom alone, which was near the top of the hotel, and he seldom had the energy to make the contact with it.

He told me that the nicest place he knew was Japan. The second best place I cannot remember, and the third was the island of Majorca off the Mediterranean coast of Spain. I never had any ambition to go to Japan, but I one day hope to visit Majorca if it is big enough to accommodate my bicycle.

When we were not actually climbing up and down the Madrid stairs, we found ourselves in a state of utter exhaustion, looking at some of the finest pictures in the world.

If I am ever made president of the Arts Council, I shall double the attendance at picture galleries, by having wheel chairs for hire at the door. Without them, no one without the stamina of a trained athlete can ever enjoy pictures to the full.

Our only restful moments were when we were watching the most gruelling game in the world — that of pelota. This marvellous spectacle, peculiar to Spain, almost atones for the Spaniards having bullfights in the same country.

But the thing that really shook Madrid was the football match between Bilbao and Valencia. Franco was there, and every bed in Madrid was taken up before we got there. We met troops of English and other people, going from place to place in search of accommodation, and finding none.

We decided to go to a neighbouring village for the night and come back to Madrid the following morning.

But we did not reckon with that king who decided to build Madrid in a desert because it happened to be in the middle of Spain, and so we searched for villages until two o'clock in the morning, and then found one with a horrible *posada*.

Those wishful thinkers who imagine that football is taking the place of bullfighting will be glad to think of the tremendous interest that was taken in this match, but from enquiries which I made at the time, it seems that bullfighting is still a much more popular spectacle.

On leaving Madrid for Zaragossa, I felt it my duty to express a few words to the proprietor of our hotel, on the subject of the shortage of essential services in the capital city. He said how sorry he was that I had been inconvenienced, but he told me that the company that supplied the electricity was English.

North Wales Guardian D / E / 2953

National Trust
Squire Yorke Explains: Why I want Erddig to be Preserved

It would appear from a letter in Friday's issue of the *Leader* that some misconception exists regarding the nature and purpose of the National Trust.

Most people know that all the houses in which the National Trust is interested have to be very highly endowed before the National Trust will take them over. If the endowment is insufficient to keep the property up to the required standard, the money has to be made up by the organisation of Summer Schools and the like.

A charge is also made for the admission of the public and there is a sum which can be drawn upon in emergencies which is subscribed by thousands of well-wishers who are interested in beauty and history. Those wishing to become members can do so by sending £2 to the National Trust, 23, Caxton Street, S.W.1, and they can then visit all the National Trust houses as often as they wish, free of charge.

Heating

At present the principal National Trust places in Wales are Powys Castle and Penrhyn Castle but the late chairman of the Council for Historic Buildings said that Erddig is the only thing of its kind in Wales and is, moreover, amongst the top 20 of all the houses in England and Wales. One of the chief experts on the subject was heard to say after visiting Erddig, 'This is my favourite country house'.

The cost of heating I can assure your correspondent is not excessive. I spend half-a-crown a day on paraffin for one stove from October to March and if I want any logs I saw them myself. In addition, I buy about one ton of coal a year for the benefit of my guests. I do not regard this as extravagant as I save in other ways, being a non-smoking, non-gambling, vegetarian tee-totaller.

No Electricity

If our heating bills are rather higher than those of the old age pensioners about whom your correspondent rightly shows concern, he may be pleased to know that we save on light, as we have no electricity. I hope moreover that he will have the same concern for me when I become an

Philip relaxing.

an old age pensioner in ten week's time.

If some of the rooms and passages get a little chill for a few periods during the winter, I feel that it is more than compensated for by the fact that the natural temperature is better for the pictures and furniture. Some of those people who have installed central heating are beginning to find out that the warm dry atmosphere tends to crack the woodwork.

As Erddig will in general only be open to the public in the summer, not much heating should ever be necessary.

The other main element which is harmful to furniture is direct sunlight, but as, out of our 365? windows, less than one in a hundred face the south, little damage is brought about in that way.

No one need worry unduly regarding the expense of maintaining the house. Erddig was so magnificently built, 300 years ago, that the cost of repairs was negligible until the National Coal Board upset the levels by taking away, without compensation, the pillar of coal on which we stood, and which I always understood was the largest in the country. I am happy to say that the Board is now co-operating splendidly and striving to make the repairs so that they will not show.

Nothing but oak was used in the building and this was grown in the woods and sawn on the premises. The sawpit and some of the original saws still remain after 300 years.

The bricks were made from a clay pit which is now a pond in the garden, and when part of the house was faced with stone, Cefn stone was used and described at the time as being 'the best in the neighbourhood.'

This is in contrast to our other house, called Dyffryn Aled, in the Vale of Clwyd, which was built of Bath stone brought all the way by a procession of horses, donkeys and mules carrying two stones apiece because the roads were not good enough for waggons, and then going back to Somerset for another load.

The Bath stone did not stand up to the Welsh climate as well as the local product and the house passed out of the family in 1912 and has now been demolished like so many others.

The Treasury has several times offered a grant to my brother and myself for the restoration of Erddig and its contents, but we have always turned it down.

No ratepayer need be concerned about the cost of the preservation of Erddig. We pay very heavy rates and in return we receive the vigilance of the police, the alertness of the fire brigade, and nothing else. If Erddig is demolished, the local rate fund will be poorer by hundreds of pounds.

Your correspondent is right in thinking that some fine houses are being saved from destruction by being converted into flats and hostels on a non-profitmaking basis, but that excellent work is being undertaken by societies other than the National Trust.

Offer

My offer to the Trust is that they shall accept the whole estate for the preservation of Erddig and its principal contents, together with an area of parkland which must be left intact. Any extra money which they require they can obtain by exploiting the property out of sight of the house.

The National Trust tell me that they seldom turn down any offer of over a million pounds, but if they decide to turn this one down, I am in the fortunate position of being able to sell the whole concern, lock, stock, and barrel, for my own personal and selfish benefit and as I have spent the greater part of my life saving for such a contingency as this, I would be able to pay the death duties on my brother's estate and still have several hundreds of pounds left over to enable me to spend the rest of my life in the comfort of the warmer climate of Spain, which I am the first person to have discovered as a holiday resort.

Enjoyment

But my real interest for many years has been that this unique establishment, for which my family have foregone many luxuries and comforts over seven generations, should now be dedicated to the enjoyment of all those who have interests beyond the bare necessities of life, who may come here and see a part of our national heritage preserved for all foreseeable time.

Anyone who wishes can step out of Wrexham and walk at will in the park, where they may be hard put to it to find anything that has not remained unaltered for hundreds of years.

About the newest item is the 'Cup and Saucer', which my great-great-grandfather constructed in 1774, and which is now being restored by voluntary labour.

Erddig is a kind of oasis in the middle of a swiftly developing industrial area, and I think there is a silent majority who hope it may always remain so.

Philip Yorke, Erddig.
Wrexham Leader 16 January 1970.

Correspondence with Horizon Holidays

Date: 23.7.61   Report No:

Dear Mr. Marnau

(1) I very much regret that I have not previously sent in the Hotel Questionaire. Lack of information is a breach that I am not often guilty of.

All I can say in mitigation is that I have seen so many letters from the office to the hotels in question that I thought you knew the facts already.

They are

              Senor Jaimie Moncho
              Hotel Victoria
              Benidorm   Tel. 120
   and   Senor Jose Moncho
              Hotel Busa
              Benidorm   Tel. 185

(2) John took some excellent photos of me last year. This year I am looking old and careworn and can hardly face the looking glass, much less the camera. In view of the present circumstances, I cannot recommend having my photo in next year's propaganda.

(3) In the past I think I have made some odd remarks in my letters and reports, but if I write them all down again it may interfere with my other work.

If you wish, however, I will come and repeat them verbally in your presence with additions if desirable, on Aug. 14th.

(3) [sic] I cannot suggest any guide book corrections as I have never read the guide book.

Thank you very much for your kind appreciation of my efforts & prompt attention. As regards the P.S. I think I can at least claim that my behaviour in this respect has been exemplary.

Please send me another tablet as soon as possible. I have nearly run out.

Yours ever
Phil.

REPRESENTATIVE'S FORTNIGHTLY REPORT
RESORT: BENIDORM
NAME: PHILIP YORKE
DATE: 5. 8. 61
REPORT NO: 8. 0?

Dear Mr Marnau

This tour seems to be going all right now, but I can assure you that it is no thanks to you.

In the first few minutes we had a major crisis because the four people booked to sit together did not regard seats 34. 33. 39. & 38 as complying with their contract. Nor do I.

After an unpleasant hold-up at the aerodrome, I managed to persuade Miss Clarkson to go and sit somewhere else, but if ever you learn anything about coach touring, you will realize that it is always best to try and start off without any loss of tempers.

Within ten minutes I was up against further trouble because there was no bath allotted to Mr Brooks. It is a bit of a racket taking money for baths anyway, as it is only at the first three hotels that the question of a bath is ever in doubt. But I suppose if people are prepared to pay an extra £1 per night for a bath, there is no harm in relieving them of it. But I think that the least you can do is to make some arrangements accordingly. If there is one thing I have mentioned more than another it is that I dislike holding up the whole party while I seek favours for individuals. It was the same thing at Burgos, and I only managed it because Mr Brooks had brought his letter with him. I suppose he did not trust us as much as the Merzes did: and with good justification.

I have only two more tours & I want you to take a little more trouble and pay attention to the job at your end.

On our arrival at Benidorm, a party of six wanted me to send them home immediately at our expense because they had booked three double rooms, and had been put into two suites of three each. I remonstrated with the manager who clearly shewed me that we had overtopped our allotment of double rooms, and he could not do anything about it. I don't blame you overmuch for that; I suppose you were just unlucky with the bookings. But remember that Napoleon said 'Give me lucky Generals'. It was late evening before I found the solution, and Mr Parkes, who is only here because he wanted to be on my tour again, most kindly consented to go into a single room, and his nephew into another. It is well known that the single rooms are not as good as the double & have no shower, and the hotel charges less for them. You may think it worth while to write him a letter of thanks for getting us out of a very difficult situation, or, of course, you may not read as far as this.

Eventually I got the party of six into a line of rooms on the first floor just above the kitchens, and they have caught the plague and are living on Vichy water and pills, and are complaining about the pains in their stomachs which they largely blame on the stink of the cooking which blows in through their windows.

There was a disgruntled man at the Victoria who will never come with us again, and his baby was ill and a mirror fell and cut his hand open and it had to be stitched and there was a storm at Barcelona & they arrived many hours late, and he is going to write you an angry letter about the whole affair. His name is Graham I think, but you need not pay too much attention to the letter as he struck me as being of the grouchy type, like you.

The invoice book which you have sent for paying the bills is perfectly ridiculous. It is filled with a conglomeration of unnecessary details in ridiculous languages, and is absurdly unwieldly. Fortunately I have my musical saw with me and I have been able to cut the book in two. This is the very best kind of economy as nobody loses by it, and the other half will do for whoever is ass enough to take on the job of working under your so-called management next year. Unfortunately I have not made the cut very straight as I think the saw wants sharpening.

I should have thought the address of H. H would have been more useful than all that rot about Letti & Giorve. I take it that the Italians dont have showers. So I suppose I have learned something from it anyway.

The Bond should fit the pocket and be as simple as possible. Last year's model was much better.

If you should wish for any help in making out next year's itinerary, you have only to let me know and I shall be only too happy to send you suggestions. But I dare say you will prefer to make it out in your own slip-shod way, and rely on the enginuity [sic] of the courier to correct your silly mistakes.

I rather think I know of someone who would like to take on the job. His name is Sean and he is well known to Ultramar who speak well of him. He has heard (not from me) that I am the best courier in the business, & that I am shortly retiring and he says that he regards that as a challenge to see whether he could not do a little better. He realizes that it is a stepdown from being a Hotel Representative to being a courier, but nevertheless I should regard his motives as adequate cause for changing his occupation. At the moment I think he works for Wings or Sky Tours or some inferior company. I don't really ever hope for much action to be taken as a result of my letters, some of which are not even being answered. I am beginning to wonder if they are even being read.

I am happy to realize, however, that if I send my communications by cablegramme, and my letters in quadruplicate, some action is taken.

D/E/2967

Correspondence with his mother

1761332
Gunner Yorke, P. S.
East Blockhouse
Angle, near Pembroke
S. Wales

17 Jan. 41

Dear Mother

One of the first questions I was asked was about my entertaining qualities, so I think I had better ask you to send the saw straight away.

There is also a peculiar roll of black velvet on a stick & two white gloves in the top left drawer of the big wardrobe in my bedroom; please put them, if you can, in the same parcel.

We arrived in rather late, but some people did not arrive until this morning & I think a few are still missing.

About four or five are from Wrexham.

The bike was accepted though it is the only one.

I met a lady in the train who is the daughter of one of the ex-brewerys in Wrexham. She used to come to Erddig as an R. C. child. Her mother touches the park near Sontley.

I am sorry to trouble you so soon with the parcel, but I think it will be useful.

Much love
Phil.

Church Army Centres for H. M. Forces
From 221 Bty RA
Cooden
Sussex

Date 15 Mar 42.

Dear Mother

The Registered letter turned out to be very dull & about coal or something, so I rushed it back to Boscawen & Richmond to deal with. How ghastly about the bone episode. We are very lucky to have Rigar in

Wrexham. I hope Sheila was not horrified to find him a black man.

Lady Thorpe knows Erddig, or did I tell you that the last time. She came over with the Marks when her husband was Professor Thorpe & I was in a cradle & she tried to stop him tickling my feet to see my toes close up to clench the branch of the rudimentary tree. She says he was most uncomfortable sitting in the saloon as he feared for the safety of the octagonal Worcester vases which were then worth £2,000. I believe the poem which we read when I was last at home was about Sir John Marks. She say she would like to see it if you would not mind making a copy of it. I wonder if a typewriter is still working.

Rumours are abroad that the Canadians may be taking over this battery. I shall be quite sorry to leave but if we are sent to Ireland it might be amusing. I am glad I brought the drums back but I shall go away sorrowfully as I have so many possessions. This is Warships week. I have invested fifty guineas in war stamps to shew that my regard for the war is greater than my fear of Mr. Davies the Bank.

Much love Phil.

WHEN REPLYING WRITE TO
address uncertain

Dear Mother

Thanks for your letter. I am glad such a lot is going on at Erddig, as I was rather afraid that you were rather cut off from the worlds activities. I understand the Spanish perfectly, but it had better now cease. I am afraid least the authorities feel that the united nations do not have the advantage of our undivided attention.

It was rather a surprise to me to find myself at Belfast, but I find that some of the people in the theatre & elsewhere still remember me. The war office has been very tactful again. When I come home I will bring the guide book.

I am glad you have taken to the Americans: if there is anyone of especial amicability, do not hesitate to let him have my bicycle. There is something a little wrong with the gears but it works alright in the middle one. I wonder if Jones could take it to the little shop on the right on the way to the Beast Market. The man should wash out all the stray bits & put it back & I will have two gears left. He need not trouble to repair it properly till the war is over.

A rather nice Canadian sergeant whom I met at a revivalist meeting in Eastbourne may come to borrow it to ride to Caernarvon. I forget his name but he has a note in my hand scrawl. He looks a tiny bit like Wil. R. Rose (He is a Plymouth brother).

I have now had to swallow my disapproval and become a Sergeant. I will tell you my proper address when I know it, but if anything urgent comes up in the meantime I dare say
Serg. Yorke P. A. E. C.
1761332
Victoria Barracks
Belfast
might find me.
Much love
Phil.

D/E/2928

Miscellaneous Correspondence

Erddig
Wrexham

16. 4. 68
Stationmaster
Wolverhampton

Dear Sir

The name signs at the end of the platform are small, too high, and they face the wrong way.

It is the people arriving by train who may wish to know when they have reached Wolverhampton, and not the folk who have the misfortune to be there already.

Yours truly
Philip Yorke

D/E/2926

Erddig Park

The Rector of Wrexham
29. 2. 72

Dear Rector

I am sorry I have been to Wrexham Church so infrequently but today I was greatly disappointed at what occured [sic].

The introit sounded to me rather puny, and I hoped that the postlude might be more acceptable, but it wasnt. (I usually miss the introit as I get late. Then we suffered from the Benedicte, which may have been all right for Shadrach, Mesach and Abednego in the fiery furnace in its longer form, but it seems to me an unnecessary form of lenten penance now that it is decapitated, and completely unacceptible [sic] for soldiers.

It would have been much better to sing *All things bright and beautiful* instead. If people do not like the third verse, leave it out (and everybody will read it anyway). One other hymn would have been enough before the sermon, which would have made up for the National Anthems. And what has happened to *Onward Christian Soldiers* and *Fight the Good Fight*?

I don't think much of the pulpit lighting, and I came on a motor bike because it is difficult to park a car.

I am not alone in regarding it as a disappointing service.

This letter requires no reply.

Yours ever

Phil

D/E/2926

How to get Britain out of the Red
(letter to the *Daily Telegraph*)

Dear Sir

May I present my recipe for getting Britain out of the nasty mess she is in.

Arms to South Africa	£100,000,000
Abolish sanctions	£100,000,000
Frigates to Spain	£100,000,000
2/- on prescriptions	£ 50,000,000
Further U.S. Beatle tour	£ 1,140,000
Total Benefit —	£371,140,000

Philip Yorke, Erddig Hall, Wrexham

Handwritten over the letter is 'Unwanted milk for overfed children £20,000,000'.

Omitted

I notice a mathematical error in my letter, published on Friday. A £20,000,000 item was unfortunately omitted.

May I mention too that the extra £140,000 added to the suggested Beatle million pound tour of the United States was to allow for devaluation.

Philip Yorke, Erddig, Wrexham

D/E/2963

An Hilarious Evening

Squire Yorke's technical knowledge is only equalled by his sense of fun and all who were present at his lantern lecture last Thursday will be for ever grateful to the Civic Society for arranging it, as well as to Mr. Yorke for coming. Mr. Donald Bond introduced him and also, with the assistance of Mr. Cooper, operated the lantern, which had been in use for a couple of generations. There were a few difficulties, such as Erddig persistently appearing upside down and its appearance rightways was greeted with applause. Edwardian pictures of the family, the dogs Bruno and Prince, the donkeys, as well as pictures of some of the priceless treasures at Erddig, were expertly commented on. The troubles with the Coal Board (it was mining that caused Erddig to be cracked) and the story of the water ram, give us a sense of intimacy with this remarkable family. The happy informality made it an evening to remember.

After the coffee interval, Mr. Yorke showed the promised colour slides, made by his father:– a kaleidoscope, a man in bed opening and shutting his mouth till a mouse jumped into it; and a man and donkey changing heads like Bottom in *Midsummer Night's Dream*. And Mr. Yorke had even brought one of his famous bicycles and rode it across the hall in style.

The lecture made a profit of £16.72 for the local Jubilee Fund.

Reprinted from the *Llangollen Broadsheet* of 5 October 1977.

Recollections of Philip Yorke

This is a selection of letters in response to an appeal in a local newspaper for recollections of the late Philip Yorke.

I have worked for the Yorke family for 40 years. Mr Philip Yorke was rarely at the hall until the sudden death of his brother. It was then that we came to know him as a gentleman although he loved doing everything for himself. Whatever he was cooking he would ask you to come and share even if you had just eaten and he didnt like you to refuse; he would really be cross.

He had some very funny ideas. He would go and buy a new shirt and put it on and then would start cutting the sleeves. By the time he had finished it was like a lace pattern. He wouldn't let one of us stitch it for him; he would always do it himself and (it) always had to be red cotton. He said that was the Yorke colour.

He had some awful ways. He couldn't bear you cleaning places, especially where he used to use. You would hardly have room in the Servants' Hall to eat or anything. There would be old wireless and televisions that he bought at a jumble sale. Many a time we would go in there he would have his motorbike all in pieces and (we) wouldn't dare touch it. He had so many funny ways. He would save a pile of empty tins and make holes in them all and thread a piece of string through and tie it to the door, and then if anybody tried to break in his dog Trixy would bark.

He was a very nervous man really. (He) didn't go to the bedrooms to sleep but had a bed in the corner of the drawing room and always kept a gun under the bed with a stocking over it, and many nights he told me he would sleep on the stairs with his dog.

He had funny ways really. Anyone mention they were looking for somewhere for a meal or sleep, many a Monday morning when we have gone in he had had someone sleep in every bed. He would make them all up himself and give them all breakfast before we got there, but we didn't know where to start clearing up.

He was a very hard-working man too. There wasn't anything he wouldn't do. He would climb on to the roofs and try prepare any leaks

which at Erddig were many, for when he moved there I think it rained in nearly every room. He even put his hand to chimney sweeping. I could say so much about him but I will stop here, but just to say there won't be another gentleman like him.
Mrs S. E. Alman, Wrexham.

I met the man only once, but the memory of it and Erddig as it was in those days has stayed with me.

The year was 1969 and I was invited to Erddig one evening to go fishing by a school friend. I well recall being impressed by the great old house, even though it was in a poor state of repair. My friend led the way to one of the windows near the staircase leading to the door. Philip Yorke was in the room and my friend asked permission to go and fish in the lake around the side of the house. The contents of that room were amazing, suits of armour, swords, pikes, and countless other objects filled it from floor to ceiling. Apparently every room in the house was in the same condition as the one I had seen.

The fishing was uneventful and we became bored, as small boys do, so we began to explore the grounds. In one of the small ornamental ponds which contained goldfish, one was floating on the surface, although still alive. I gave the fish the kiss of life, put it back into the pond and watched amazed as it swam off. Shortly after Philip Yorke came out of the house. It was fascinating to me to see the sheep which had been grazing on the lawn all run up to him as dogs would do. Mr Yorke then came down to talk to us and told us a little about the treasures in the house. My friend was full of my saving of the goldfish and told him all about it. Mr Yorke praised me and promised to tell my school how clever I had been. I don't know whether he did or not, but I was grateful for just having met him.

Mr Yorke then walked with us around the lake, followed by his sheep. He then invited us to take a rowing boat out onto the lake and to return whenever we wished. At this he returned inside the house and I never saw him again.
Dave Taylor, Rhewl, Mostyn.

My friend Barbara and I were walking through Erddig, as we often did as children. I was about 11 years old at that time. We were near the Cup and Saucer one beautiful warm sunny evening when Philip Yorke

Philip with the actress Gwen Nelson.

approached us; he was very friendly. As we passed the time of day with him Barbara was desperately trying to attract my attention and it wasn't until he turned to walk away that she told me he was wearing odd shoes, one black, one brown. As youngsters we couldn't stop laughing, we had never seen the like before.
(Mrs) Keris Bates, Wrexham.

I have fond recollections of Philip Yorke and his many eccentricities. We had a small TV repair business in the village of Rhos, and Squire Yorke was a frequent visitor, him and his little dog. I was quite amused to find when carrying something out to the car, he had removed all but the driver's seat so the dog could move around.

Also he owned property in Ruabon and he had two tenants and one TV aerial. He came to our shop for a very long length of co-axial cable. When we asked him why he needed such a length, he said 'Well, when I attach a brick to it, to throw it over the roof, as the other tenants have their TV in the rear of the house'!! He was so fond of Spain and anything Spanish. One time he bought a small battery-operated razor with a carrying case and mirror combined. A few months later he came in the shop to buy another one, so I asked if he'd lost the original one. 'Oh no', he replied, 'I've still got the razor but I've lost the mirror'.

At the small church on his estate at Penylan, there was no heating, so he'd take his own little paraffin stove and hide it under his coat. Well, if it was a long sermon he would fall asleep and the stove would start smoking, and it would look as if he'd caught fire and the children would delight in beating his coat. This is the little church where he actually died, very peacefully, so much so that until the end of the sermon people assumed he had just fallen asleep. Such a nice end for a very nice man.*
Diana Lewis, Acrefair.

---

* Philip died before the service began. Penylan is in fact on the Ormrod estate.

I recently read your letter about Mr Philip Yorke in the *Wrexham Leader*.

He occasionally used to preach at our church and tell us of his experiences in Spain. He said travel was quite cheap if one did not mind sitting upon and lying between the orange boxes on board ship.

Once he was in a concert locally, playing his musical saw and asked me to accompany him on the piano ... he was so close during our rehearsals that I was deaf in my left ear for three weeks afterwards.

One afternoon he called, so we invited him to stay for tea; he asked for a second slice of sandwich cake as he had never had any before. He decided to come to church so said he had better go home and tell his housekeeper he had eaten. My mother was convinced he was going home to change but I knew better. Sure enough, he came back just as he had been, pullover inside out with his tie on the outside! He came back after church and asked what time we were having supper — out of luck as we had none.

On many an occasion, I saw him in the bank and asking for the dirtiest notes they could find. He told us he used to go into a supermarket and ask what they were giving away. When told there was nothing, but peas was a cheap line that week, he used to stock up with those ...

A former colleague said he often invited people down to the hall and 'played' follow the leader all through the rooms and over the bed.

I think that despite his wealth he was lonely as he often called by on the non-wealthy of the community (and that includes ourselves!) and one Christmas he knocked a neighbour's door as their house looked so warm and welcoming — they had a decorated Christmas tree by their window.

Priscilla Hughes, Eyton, Wrexham.

My family had such happy childhood memories of the Yorkes and Erddig. We were tenants of Simon at Coed-y-Glyn so saw quite a lot of both. Simon, Phil, and their mother — in fact they were like elderly cousins and so very kind to us. We were allowed to ride our ponies all over their parks and woods and on occasions we were asked to tea — to skate in the winter on the canal, and a formal tea with Simon in the dining room, or in summer it was to pick strawberries, and tea on the lawn with Phil and Mrs Yorke. Phil would play the organ afterwards or put on the polyphon and Mrs Yorke would show us how to dance the minuet. Another time it was a rabbit hunt under the very overgrown roses — ending in a dogfight between the Yorke terrier (Sealyham?) and our lurcher. Phil rushed to fetch a bucket of water and the pepper to throw over the dogs!

Phil would arrive for lunch on his penny-farthing. (He was so proud of having ridden it all over Ireland when on an acting tour). Our other guests couldn't even ride it on the lawn!

When the coal allowance from Bersham Colliery didn't quite last the year, Phil would arrive in his old Ford (!) and borrow from us, but we would have to go back to Erddig with him, and push the car up the hill … .

When the Pony Club had a rally in the park, Phil supplied the music for Musical Chairs by playing the trombone! …

When during the war a bomb was dropped near Coed-y-Glyn my mother decided to take us to live in Scotland with my grandmother … . We returned to the area in 1944 and so were able to enjoy the Yorke brothers again. Phil lent his tandem bike to my teenage twin brothers. This time tea was in the kitchen at Erddig, and Phil called his other guest (a retired actor, who was cutting the undergrowth down at the end of the garden) by blowing on his French Horn. He'd taken this man to see the film Dr Zhivago so he would know how to act the part of a Russian serf and put a sickle to good use at Erddig. Phil used to sleep in a different room every night so if anyone broke into Erddig, they wouldn't know where he was … . Both Simon and Phil were the kindest of men.

Maureen Owen (née Ormrod), Sydney, Australia.